Best Stories of Ambrose Bierce

Abridged Version

V&S PUBLISHERS

Published by:

F-2/16, Ansari road, Daryaganj, New Delhi-110002
☎ 23240026, 23240027 • *Fax:* 011-23240028
Email: info@vspublishers.com • *Website:* www.vspublishers.com

Regional Office : Hyderabad
5-1-707/1, Brij Bhawan (Beside Central Bank of India Lane)
Bank Street, Koti, Hyderabad - 500 095
☎ 040-24737290
E-mail: vspublishershyd@gmail.com

Branch Office : Mumbai
Jaywant Industrial Estate, 2nd Floor-222, Tardeo Road
Opposite Sobo Central, Mumbai - 400 034
☎ 022-23510736
E-mail: vspublishersmum@gmail.com

Follow us on:

All books available at **www.vspublishers.com**

© Copyright: V&S Publishers
Edition 2017

The Copyright of this book, as well as all matter contained herein (including illustrations) rests with the Publishers. No person shall copy the name of the book, its title design, matter and illustrations in any form and in any language, totally or partially or in any distorted form. Anybody doing so shall face legal action and will be responsible for damages.

Printed at: Repro Knowledgecast Ltd., Thane.

Publisher's Note

It has been our constant endeavour at the **V&S Publishers** to publish all kinds of books ranging from Fiction, Non-fiction, Storybooks, Children Encyclopaedias, to Self-Help, Science Books, Dictionaries, Grammar Books, Self-Development, Management Books, etc.

However, this is for the first time that we are venturing into the vast, rich and fathomless ocean of English Literature and have come up with a this book authored by Ambrose Bierce. There is a lot to learn from this writing style, selection of plot, development and building of theme and suspense of the story, emphasis and presentation of characters, dialogues, working towards the climax of the story, presenting the climax, and then finally concluding the story.

Besides the above mentioned characteristics, the book contain a short biography of the author, his brief life history, notable works and literary achievements. Each story has a set of word meanings on each page.

These books are not only a boon for the school-going students, particularly studying in senior classes from the seventh standard till the twelfth, but are also a treasure trove for all those young and aspiring writers, voracious readers and lovers of English language and literature.

Contents

Publisher's Note 3
Biograohy of Ambrose Bierce 7
One of Twins 10
Moxon's Master 18
On Summer Night 29
My Favourite Murder 33
John Mortonson's Funeral 41
John Bartine's Watch 45
An Inhabitant of Carcosa 51
An Occurrence at Out Greek Bridge 57
The Realm of The Unreal 67
APsychological Shipwreck 77
The Boby Tramp 82
The Secret of Macarger's Gulch 89
The Moonlit Road 96
The Haunted Valley 107
The Death of HAlpin Frayser 118

Ambrose Gwinnett Bierce

Born on June 24, 1842
Died on sometime after December 26, 1913
Notable Works: *The Fiend's Delight, The Devil's Dictionary, The Cynic's Word Book, Collected Works* and a number of ghost stories and realistic and short war stories, such as: 'An Occurrence at Owl Creek Bridge', 'The Boarded Window', 'Killed at Resaca', and 'Chickamauga'. He also published several volumes of poetry like the *Fantastic Fables.* He published a column called 'Prattle' and became one of the first regular columnists and editorialists to be employed on William Randolph Hearst's newspaper, the *San Francisco Examiner*,
Honours: At least three films have been made of Bierce's story, 'An Occurrence at Owl Creek Bridge'. A silent film version, *The Bridge*, was made in 1929. A French version called *La Rivière du Hibou*, directed by Robert Enrico, was released in 1962 and another version, directed by Brian James Egen, was released in 2005.

Early life

Ambrose Gwinnett Bierce, an American editorialist, journalist, short story writer, fabulist and satirist was born on June 24, 1842. Bierce was born at Horse Cave Creek in Meigs County, Ohio to Marcus Aurelius Bierce and Laura Sherwood Bierce. His parents were a poor, but literary couple who instilled in him a deep love for books and writing. The boy grew up in Kosciusko County, Indiana, attending high school at the county seat, Warsaw.

Military Career

At the outset of the American Civil War, Bierce enlisted in the Union Army's 9th Indiana Infantry Regiment. He participated in the Operations in Western Virginia campaign (1861), and was present at the "first battle" at Philippi. He received newspaper attention for his daring rescue, under fire, of a gravely wounded comrade at the Battle of Rich Mountain. In February 1862, he was commissioned First Lieutenant, and served on the staff of General William Babcock Hazen as a topographical engineer, making maps of likely battlefields.

Bierce fought at the Battle of Shiloh (April 1862), a terrifying experience that became a source for several later short stories and the memoir, 'What I Saw of Shiloh'. Bierce received the rank of *brevet major* before resigning from the Army.

Journalistic Career

Bierce remained in San Francisco for many years, eventually becoming famous as a contributor and/or editor for a number of local newspapers and periodicals, including

The San Francisco News Letter, *The Argonaut*, the *Overland Monthly*, *The Californian* and *The Wasp*. A selection of his crime reporting from *The San Francisco News Letter* was included in The Library of America anthology *True Crime*.

Literary Works and Achievements

Bierce was considered **a master of pure English** by his contemporaries, and virtually everything that came from his pen was notable for its judicious wording and economy of style. He wrote in a variety of literary genres.

Bierce lived and wrote in England from 1872 to 1875, contributing to *Fun* magazine. His first book, *The Fiend's Delight*, a compilation of his articles, was published in London in 1873 by John Camden Hotten under the pseudonym, "Dod Grile. Returning to the United States, he again took up residence in San Francisco. From 1879 to 1880, he travelled to Rockerville and Deadwood in the Dakota Territory, to try his hand as local manager for a New York mining company, but when the company failed he, returned to San Francisco and resumed his career in journalism.

In 1887, he published a column called 'Prattle' and became one of the first regular columnists and editorialists to be employed on William Randolph Hearst's newspaper, the *San Francisco Examiner*, eventually becoming one of the most prominent and influential among the writers and journalists of the West Coast. He remained associated with Hearst Newspapers until 1906.

His short stories are held among the best of the 19th century, providing a popular following based on his roots. He wrote realistically of the terrible things he had seen in the war in such stories as "An Occurrence at Owl Creek Bridge", "The Boarded Window", "Killed at Resaca", and "Chickamauga". In addition to his ghost and war stories, he also published several volumes of poetry. His *Fantastic Fables* anticipated the ironic style of grotesquerie that became a more common genre in the 20th century.

One of Bierce's most famous works is his much-quoted book, *The Devil's Dictionary*, originally an occasional newspaper item which was first published in book form in 1906 as *The Cynic's Word Book*. It consists of satirical definitions of English words and political double-talk.Bierce's twelve-volume, *Collected Works* were published in 1909, the seventh volume of which consists solely of *The Devil's Dictionary*, the title Bierce himself preferred to *The Cynic's Word Book.*

Writing Style

Despite his reputation as a searing critic, Bierce was known to encourage younger writers, including poet George Sterling and fiction writer W. C. Morrow. Bierce had a distinctive style of writing, especially in his stories. His style often embraces **an abrupt beginning, dark imagery, vague references to time, limited descriptions, impossible events** and the **theme of war.**

Disappearance
In October 1913, the 71-year old Bierce, departed to Washington, D.C., for a tour of his old Civil War battlefields. By December, he had proceeded through Louisiana and Texas, crossing by way of El Paso into Mexico, which was in the throes of revolution. Bierce travelled to Mexico to gain a first-hand experience of the Mexican Revolution. While traveling with the rebel troops, he disappeared without a trace.

Trivia
Ambrose Gwinnett Bierce was the tenth of the thirteen children that his parents had, and his father gave all of them names beginning with the letter, "A".

One Of Twins

— Ambrose Bierce

A letter found among the papers of the late Mortimer Barr

YOu ask me if in my experience as one of a pair of twins I ever observed anything unaccountable by the natural laws with which we have acquaintance. As to that you shall judge; perhaps we have not all acquaintance with the same natural laws. You may know some that I do not, and what is to me unaccountable may be very clear to you.

You knew my brother John -- that is, you knew him when you knew that I was not present; but neither you nor, I believe, any human being could distinguish between him and me if we chose to seem alike. Our parents could not; ours is the only instance of which I have any knowledge of so close resemblance as that. I speak of my brother John, but I am not at all sure that his name was not Henry and mine John. We were regularly christened, but afterward, in the very act of tattooing us with small distinguishing marks, the operator lost his reckoning; and although I bear upon my forearm a small 'H' and he bore a 'J,' it is by no means certain that the letters ought not to have been transposed. During our boyhood our parents tried to distinguish us more obviously by our clothing and other simple devices, but we would so frequently exchange suits and otherwise circumvent the enemy that they abandoned all such ineffectual attempts, and during all the years that we lived together at home everybody recognized the difficult of the situation and made the best of it by calling us both 'Jehnry.' I have often wondered at my father's forbearance in not branding us conspicuously upon our unworthy brows, but as we were tolerably good boys and used our power of embarrassment and annoyance with commendable moderation, we escaped the iron. My father was, in fact, a singularly good-natured man, and I think quietly enjoyed nature's practical joke.

Soon after we had come to California, and settled at San Jose (where the only good fortune that awaited us was our meeting with so kind a friend as you), the family, as you know, was broken up by the death of both my parents in the same week. My father died insolvent, and the homestead was

Acquaintance – *Associate,*
Desert - *Forsake utt rly*
Distinguish – *Differentiate*
Commendable – *Praiseworthy*
Insolvent *– Bankrupt, Pneniless*

sacrificed to pay his debts. My sisters returned to relatives in the East, but owing to your kindness John and I, then twenty-two years of age, obtained employment in San Francisco, in different quarters of the town. Circumstances did not permit us to live together, and we saw each other infrequently, sometimes not oftener than once a week. As we had few acquaintances in common, the fact of our extraordinary likeness was little known. I come now to the matter of your inquiry

One day soon after we had come to this city I was walking down Market Street late in the afternoon, when I was accosted by a well-dressed man of middle age, who after greeting me cordially said, 'Stevens, I know, of course, that you do not go out much, but I have told my wife about you, and she would be glad to see you at the house. I have a notion, too, that my girls are worth knowing. Suppose you come out tomorrow at six and dine with us, en famille; and then if the ladies can't amuse you afterwards I'll stand in with a few games of billiards.'

This was said with so bright a smile and so engaging a manner that I had not the heart to refuse, and although I had never seen the man in my life I promptly replied, 'You are very good, sir, and it will give me great pleasure to accept the invitation. Please present my compliments to Mrs. Margovan and ask her to expect me.'

With a shake of the hand and a pleasant parting word, the man passed on. That he had mistaken me for my brother was plain enough. That was an error to which I was accustomed and which it was not my habit to rectify unless the matter seemed important. But how had I known that this man's name was Margovan? It certainly is not a name that one would apply to a man at random, with a probability that it would be right. In point of fact, the name was as strange to me as the man.

The next morning I hastened to where my brother was employed and met him coming out of the offic with a number of bills that he was to collect. I told him how I had 'committed' him and added that if he didn't care to keep the engagement I should be delighted to continue the impersonation. 'That's queer,' he said thoughtfully. 'Margovan is the only man in the offic here whom I know well and like. When he came in this morning and we had passed the usual greetings some singular impulse prompted me to say, "Oh, I beg your pardon,

Debt – *Dues*
Permit – *License, To allow*
Pleasure – *Desire*
Rectify – *Correct*

Mr. Margovan, but I neglected to ask your address." I got the address, but what under the sun I was to do with it, I did not know until now. It's good of you to offer to take the consequence of your impudence, but I'll eat that dinner myself, if you please.'

He ate a number of dinners at the same place -- more than were good for him, I may add without disparaging their quality; for he fell in love with Miss Margovan, proposed marriage to her and was heartlessly accepted.

Several weeks after I had been informed of the engagement, but before it had been convenient for me to make the acquaintance of the young woman and her family, I met one day on Kearney Street a handsome but somewhat dissipated-looking man. Something prompted me to follow and watch, which I did without any scruple whatever. He turned up Geary Street and followed it until he came to Union Square. There he looked at his watch, then entered the square. He loitered about the paths for some time, evidently waiting for some one. Presently he was joined by a fashionably dressed and beautiful young woman and the two walked away up Stockton Street, with me following. I now felt the necessity of extreme caution, for although the girl was a stranger, it seemed to me that she would recognize me at a glance. They made several turns from one street to another and finally, after both had taken a hasty look all about -- which I narrowly evaded by stepping into a doorway -- they entered a house of which I do not care to state the location. Its location was better than its character.

I protest that my action in playing the spy upon these two strangers was without assignable motive. It was one of which I might or might not be ashamed, according to my estimate of the character of the person finding it out. As an essential part of a narrative educed by your question it is related here without hesitancy or shame.

A week later John took me to the house of his prospective father-in-law, and in Miss Margovan, as you have already surmised, but to my profound astonishment, I recognized the heroine of that discreditable adventure. A gloriously beautiful heroine of a discreditable adventure I must in justice admit that she was; but that fact has only this importance: her beauty was such a surprise to me that it cast a doubt upon her identity with the young woman I had seen before; how could the

Impudence – *Boldness*
Scruple – *Restraint Misgiving*
Loiter – *Wander*
Caution – *Carefulness*
Surmise – *Imagine, Suspect, Guess*

marvellous fascination of her face have failed to strike me at that time? But no -- there was no possibility of error; the difference was due to costume, light and general surroundings.

John and I passed the evening at the house, enduring, with the fortitude of long experience, such delicate enough banter as our likeness naturally suggested. When the young lady and I were left alone for a few minutes I looked her squarely in the face and said with sudden gravity,

'You, too, Miss Margovan, have a double. I saw her last Tuesday afternoon in Union Square.'

She trained her great grey eyes upon me for a moment, but her glance was a trifle less steady than my own and she withdrew it, fixing it on the tip of her shoe.

'Was she very like me?' she asked, with an indifference which I thought a little o erdone.

'So like,' said I, 'that I greatly admired her, and being unwilling to lose sight of her I confess that I followed her until -- Miss Margovan, are you sure that you understand?'

She was now pale, but entirely calm. She again raised her eyes to mine, with a look that did not falter.

'What do you wish me to do?' she asked. 'You need not fear to name your terms. I accept them.'

It was plain, even in the brief time given me for reflection, that in dealing with this girl ordinary methods would not do, and ordinary exactions were needless.

'Miss Margovan,' I said, doubtless with something of the compassion in my voice that I had in my heart, 'it is impossible not to think you the victim of some horrible compulsion. Rather than impose new embarrassments upon you I would prefer to aid you to regain your freedom.'

She shook her head, sadly and hopelessly, and I continued, with agitation,

'Your beauty unnerves me. I am disarmed by your frankness and your distress. If you are free to act upon conscience you will, I believe, do what you conceive to be best; if you are not -- well, Heaven help us all! You have nothing to fear from me but such opposition to this marriage as I can try to justify on -- on other grounds.'

These were not my exact words, but that was the sense of them, as nearly as my sudden and conflicting emotions

Fortitude – *Strength*
Banter – *Teasing*
Aid – *Help*
Distress – *Pain*
Justify – *Defend*

permitted me to express it. I rose and left her without another look at her, met the others as they re-entered the room and said, as calmly as I could, 'I have been bidding Miss Margovan good evening; it is later than I thought.'

John decided to go with me. In the street he asked if I had observed anything singular in Julia's manner.

'I thought her ill,' I replied; 'that is why I left.' Nothing more was said.

The next evening I came late to my lodgings. The events of the previous evening had made me nervous and ill; I had tried to cure myself and attain to clear thinking by walking in the open air, but I was oppressed with a horrible presentiment of evil -- a presentiment which I could not formulate. It was a chill, foggy night; my clothing and hair were damp and I shook with cold. In my dressing gown and slippers before a blazing grate of coals I was even more uncomfortable. I no longer shivered but shuddered -- there is a difference. The dread of some impending calamity was so strong and dispiriting that I tried to drive it away by inviting a real sorrow -- tried to dispel the conception of a terrible future by substituting the memory of a painful past. I recalled the death of my parents and endeavoured to fix my mind upon the last sad scenes at their bedsides and their graves. It all seemed vague and unreal, as having occurred ages ago and to another person. Suddenly, striking through my thought and parting it as a tense cord is parted by the stroke of steel -- I can think of no other comparison -- I heard a sharp cry as of one in mortal agony! The voice was that of my brother and seemed to come from the street outside my window. I sprang to the window and threw it open. A street lamp directly opposite threw a wan and ghastly light upon the wet pavement and the fronts of the houses. A single policeman, with upturned collar, was leaning against a gatepost, quietly smoking a cigar. No one else was in sight. I closed the window and pulled down the shade, seated myself before the fire and tried to fix my mind upon my surroundings. By way of assisting, by performance of some familiar act, I looked at my watch; it marked half-past eleven. Again I heard that awful cry! It seemed in the room -- at my side. I was frightened and for some moments had not the power to move. A few minutes later -- I have no recollection of the intermediate

Oppress – *Supress, Dominate*
Dread – *Fear*
Dispel – *Dismiss, Alleviate*
Wan – *Pale*
Intermediate – *Middle*

time -- I found myself hurrying along an unfamiliar street as fast as I could walk. I did not know where I was, nor whither I was going, but presently sprang up the steps of a house before which were two or three carriages and in which were moving lights and a subdued confusion of voices. It was the house of Mr. Margovan.

You know, good friend, what had occurred there. In one chamber lay Julia Margovan, hours dead by poison; in another John Stevens, bleeding from a pistol wound in the chest, inflicted by his own hand. As I burst into the room; pushed aside the physicians and laid my hand upon his forehead, he unclosed his eyes, stared blankly, closed them slowly and died without a sign.

I knew no more until six weeks afterwards, when I had been nursed back to life by your own saintly wife in your own beautiful home. All of that you know, but what you do not know is this -- which, however, has no bearing upon the subject of your psychological researches -- at least not upon that branch of them in which, with a delicacy and consideration all your own, you have asked for less assistance than I think I have given you,

One moonlight night several years afterwards I was passing through Union Square. The hour was late and the square deserted. Certain memories of the past naturally came into my mind as I came to the spot where I had once witnessed that fateful assignation, and with that unaccountable perversity which prompts us to dwell upon thoughts of the most painful character I seated myself upon one of the benches to indulge them. A man entered the square and came along the walk towards me. His hands were clasped behind him, his head was bowed; he seemed to observe nothing. As he approached the shadow in which I sat I recognized him as the man whom I had seen meet Julia Margovan years before at that spot. But he was terribly altered -- grey, worn, and haggard. Dissipation and vice were in evidence in every look; illness was no less apparent. His clothing was in disorder, his hair fell across his forehead in a derangement which was at once uncanny, and picturesque. He looked fitte for restraint than liberty -- the restraint of a hospital.

With no defined purpose I rose and confronted him. He raised his head and looked me full in the face. I have no words to describe the ghastly change that came over his own; it was

Subdue – *Pacify*
Inflict *Impose*
Dwell – *Reside*
Indulge – *Pamper*
Vice – *Evil*
Uncanny – *Weird*

a look of unspeakable terror -- he thought himself eye to eye with a ghost. But he was a courageous man. 'Damn you, John Stevens!' he cried, and lifting his trembling arm he dashed his fist feebly at my face and fell headlong upon the gravel as I walked away.

Somebody found him there, stone-dead. Nothing more is known of him, not even his name. To know of a man that he is dead should be enough.

Food For Thought

Who do you think killed Henry's twin brother, John Stevens and why? How did Julia Margovan die? What happened several years later in a moon-lit night? What message do you get from the story?

Feeble – *Weak*

Moxon's Master
— Ambrose Bierce

'Are you serious? -- do you really believe that a machine thinks?'

I got no immediate reply; Moxon was apparently intent upon the coals in the grate, touching them deftly here and there with the fire-poker till they signified a sense of his attention by a brighter glow. For several weeks I had been observing in him a growing habit of delay in answering even the most trivial of commonplace questions. His air, however, was that of preoccupation rather than deliberation: one might have said that he had 'something on his mind.'

Presently he said,

'What is a "machine"? The word has been variously defined. Here is one definition from a popular dictionary: "Any instrument or organization by which power is applied and made effecti e, or a desired effect produced." Well, then, is not a man a machine? And you will admit that he thinks -- or thinks he thinks.'

'If you do not wish to answer my question,' said, rather testily, 'why not say so? -- all that you say is mere evasion. You know well enough that when I say "machine" I do not mean a man, but something that man has made and controls.'

'When it does not control him,' he said, rising abruptly and looking out of a window, whence nothing was visible in the blackness of a stormy night. A moment later he turned about and with a smile said, 'I beg your pardon; I had no thought of evasion. I considered the dictionary man's unconscious testimony suggestive and worth something in the discussion. I can give your question a direct answer easily enough, I do believe that a machine thinks about the work that it is doing.'

That was direct enough, certainly. It was not altogether pleasing, for it tended to confirm a sad suspicion that Moxon's devotion to study and work in his machine-shop had not been good for him. I knew, for one thing, that he suffered from insomnia, and that is no light affliction Had it affected his mind? His reply to my question seemed to me then evidence that it had; perhaps I should think differently about it now. I was younger then, and among the blessings that are not

---

Apparently - *Easily understable*
Fire-poker - *A metal instrument used to handle fire or charcoal*
Preoccupation - *Being very busy*
Abruptly - *Suddenly*
Machine-Shop - *A workshop in which metals are cut and shaped*

denied to youth is ignorance. Incited by that great stimulant to controversy, I said,

'And what, pray, does it think with -- in the absence of a brain?'

The reply, coming with less than his customary delay, took his favourite form of counter-interrogation, 'With what does a plant think -- in the absence of a brain?'

'Ah, plants also belong to the philosopher class! I should be pleased to know some of their conclusions; you may omit the premises.'

'Perhaps,' he replied, apparently unaffected by my foolish irony, 'you may be able to infer their convictions from their acts. I will spare you the familiar examples of the sensitive mimosa, the several insectivorous flo ers and those whose stamens bend down and shake their pollen upon the entering bee in order that it may fertilize their distant mates. But observe this. In an open spot in my garden I planted a climbing vine. When it was barely above the surface I set a stake into the soil a yard away.

The vine at once made for it, but as it was about to reach it after several days I removed it a few feet. The vine at once altered its course, making an acute angle, and again made for the stake. This manoeuvre was repeated several times, but finally, as if discouraged, the vine abandoned the pursuit and ignoring further attempts to divert it, travelled to a small tree, farther away, which it climbed.

'Roots of the eucalyptus will prolong themselves incredibly in search of moisture. A well-known horticulturist relates that one entered an old drain pipe and followed it until it came to a break, where a section of the pipe had been removed to make way for a stone wall that had been built across its course. The root left the drain and followed the wall until it found an opening where a stone had fallen out. It crept through and following the other side of the wall back to the drain, entered the unexplored part and resumed its journey.'

'And all this?'

'Can you miss the significance of it? It shows the consciousness of plants. It proves that they think.' 'Even if it did -- what then? We were speaking, not of plants, but of machines. They may be composed partly of wood -- wood that

Vine - *A grape plant*
Ignorance - *Lack of knowledge*
Horticulturist - *A person studying the science of cultivating plants*
Manoeuvre - *Deceptive plan/action*

has no longer vitality -- or wholly of metal. Is thought also an attribute of the mineral kingdom?'

'How else do you explain the phenomena, for example, of crystallization?'

'I do not explain them.'

'Because you cannot without affirmin what you wish to deny, namely, intelligent co-operation, among the constituent elements of the crystals. When soldiers form lines, or hollow squares, you call it reason. When wild geese in flight take the form of a letter V you say instinct. When the homogeneous atoms of a mineral, moving freely in solution, arrange themselves into shapes mathematically perfect, or particles of frozen moisture into the symmetrical and beautiful forms of snowflakes, you have nothing to say. You have not even invented a name to conceal your heroic unreason.'

Moxon was speaking with unusual animation and earnestness. As he paused I heard in an adjoining room known to me as his 'machine-shop,' which no one but he himself was permitted to enter, a singular thumping sound, as of someone pounding upon a table with an open hand. Moxon heard it at the same moment and, visibly agitated, rose and hurriedly passed into the room whence it came.

I thought it odd that anyone else should be in there, and my interest in my friend -- with doubtless a touch of unwarrantable curiosity -- led me to listen intently, though, I am happy to say, not at the keyhole. There were confused sounds, as of a struggle or scuffle; the floor shoo

I distinctly heard hard breathing and a hoarse whisper which said 'Damn you!' Then all was silent, and presently Moxon reappeared and said, with a rather sorry smile.

'Pardon me for leaving you so abruptly. I have a machine in there that lost its temper and cut up rough.'

Fixing my eyes steadily upon his left cheek, which was traversed by four parallel excoriations showing blood, I said,

'How would it do to trim its nails?' I could have spared myself the jest; he gave it no attention, but seated himself in the chair that he had left and resumed the interrupted monologue as if nothing had occurred,

'Doubtless you do not hold with those (I need not name them to a man of your reading) who have taught that every

Crystallisation - *To form/cause to form crystals*
Symmetrical - *Well-proportioned*
Vitality - *Vigour*
Att ibute - *Assign, Impute to*

matter is sentient, that e ery atom is a living, feeling, conscious being. I do. There is no such thing as dead, inert matter.

It is all alive; all instinct with force, actual and potential; all sensitive to the same forces in its environment and susceptible to the contagion of higher and subtler ones residing in such superior organisms as it may be brought into relation with, as those of man when he is fashioning it into an instrument of his will.

It absorbs something of his intelligence and purpose -- more of them in proportion to the complexity of the resulting machine and that of its work.

'Do you happen to recall Herbert Spencer's definition of "Life"? I read it thirty years ago. He may have altered it afterward, for anything I know, but in all that time I have been unable to think of a single word that could profitably be changed or added or removed. It seems to me not only the best defin- tion, but the only possible one.

'"Life," he says, "is a definite combination of heterogeneous changes, both simultaneous and successive, in correspondence with external co-existences and sequences."'

'That defines the phenomenon,' I said, 'but gives no hint of its cause.'

'That,' he replied, 'is all that any definition can do. As Mill points out, we know nothing of cause except as an antecedent -- nothing of effect except as a consequent. Of certain phenomena, one never occurs without another, which is dissimilar: the first in point of time we call cause, the second, effect. One who had many times seen a rabbit pursued by a dog, and had never seen rabbits and dogs otherwise, would think the rabbit the cause of the dog.

'But I fear,' he added, laughing naturally enough, 'that my rabbit is leading me a long way from the track of my legitimate quarry. I'm indulging in the pleasure of the chase for its own sake.

What I want you to observe is that in Herbert Spencer's definition of "life" the activity of a machine is included -- there is nothing in the definition that is not applicable to it. According to this sharpest of observers and deepest of thinkers, if a man during his period of activity is alive, so is a machine when in operation. As an inventor and constructor of machines I know that to be true.'

Contagion - *A contagious disease*
Antecedent - *Preceding*
Indulging - *Allowing*
Sentient - *Having senses, Conscious*

Moxon was silent for a long time, gazing absently into the fire. It was growing late and I thought it time to be going, but somehow I did not like the notion of leaving him in that isolated house, all alone except for the presence of some person of whose nature my conjectures could go no further than that it was unfriendly, perhaps malign. Leaning towards him and looking earnestly into his eyes while making a motion with my hand through the door of his workshop, I said,

'Moxon, whom have you in there?'

Somewhat to my surprise he laughed lightly and answered without hesitation,

'Nobody; the incident that you have in mind was caused by my folly in leaving a machine in action with nothing to act upon, while I undertook the interminable task of enlightening your understanding. Do you happen to know that consciousness is the creature of rhythm?'

'O bother them both!' I replied, rising and laying hold of my overcoat. 'I'm going to wish you good night; and I'll add the hope that the machine which you inadvertently left in action will have her gloves on the next time you think it needful to stop her.'

Without waiting to observe the effect of my shot I left the house.

Rain was falling, and the darkness was intense. In the sky beyond the crest of a hill towards which I groped my way along precarious plank sidewalks and across miry, unpaved streets I could see the faint glow of the city's lights, but behind me nothing was visible but a single window of Moxon's house. It glowed with what seemed to me a mysterious and fateful meaning.

I knew it was an uncurtained aperture in my friend's 'machine-shop,' and I had little doubt that he had resumed the studies interrupted by his duties as my instructor in mechanical consciousness and the fatherhood of rhythm. Odd, and in some degree humorous, as his convictions seemed to me at that time,

I could not wholly divest myself of the feeling that they had some tragic relation to his life and character -- perhaps to his destiny -- although I no longer entertained the notion that they were the vagaries of a disordered mind. Whatever might be thought of his views, his exposition of

Hesitation - *Indecision*
Folly - *Mistake*
Malign - *Defame*
Conviction - *Fixed/Firm beliefs*
Divest - *To sell off, Strip, Deprive*

them was too logical for that. Over and over, his last words came back to me, 'consciousness is the creature of rhythm.' Bald and terse as the statement was, I now found it infinitely alluring.

At each recurrence it broadened in meaning and deepened in suggestion. Why, here (I thought) is something upon which to found a philosophy. If consciousness is the product of rhythm all things are conscious, for all have motion, and all motion is rhythmic. I wondered if Moxon knew the significance and breadth of his thought -- the scope of this momentous generalization; or had he arrived at his philosophic faith by the tortuous and uncertain road of observation?

That faith was then new to me, and all Moxon's expounding had failed to make me a convert; but now it seemed as if a great light shone about me, like that which fell upon Saul of Tarsus; and out there in the storm and darkness and solitude I experienced what Lewes calls 'The endless variety and excitement of philosophic thought.' I exulted in a new sense of knowledge, a new pride of reason. My feet seemed hardly to touch the earth; it was as if I were uplifted and borne through the air by invisible wings.

Yielding to an impulse to seek further light from him whom I now recognized as my master and guide, I had unconsciously turned about, and almost before I was aware of having done so found myself again at Moxon's door. I was drenched with rain, but felt no discomfort. Unable in my excitement to find the doorbell I instinctively tried the knob. It turned and, entering, I mounted the stairs to the room that I had so recently left.

All was dark and silent; Moxon, as I had supposed, was in the adjoining room -- the 'machine-shop.' Groping along the wall until found the communicating door I knocked loudly several times, but got no response, which I attributed to the uproar outside, for the wind was blowing a gale and dashing the rain against the thin walls in sheets.

Destiny - *Fate*
Alluring - *Tempting*
Instinctively - *Spontaneously*
Groping - *To feel about with the hands*
Gale - *A very strong wind*

The drumming upon the shingle roof spanning the unceiled room was loud and incessant. I had never been invited into the machine-shop, indeed, had been denied admittance as had all others, with one exception, a skilled metal worker, of whom no one knew anything except that his name was Haley and his habit silence. But in my spiritual exaltation, discretion and civility were alike forgotten, and I opened the door. What I saw took all philosophical speculation out of me in short order.

Moxon sat facing me at the farther side of a small table upon which a single candle made all the light that was in the room. Opposite him, his back toward me, sat another person. On the table between the two was a chess-board; the men were playing. I knew little of chess, but as only a few pieces were on the board it was obvious that the game was near its close.

Moxon was intensely interested -- not so much, it seemed to me, in the game as in his antagonist, upon whom he had fixed so intent a look that, standing though I did directly in the line of his vision, I was altogether unobserved. His face was ghastly white, and his eyes glittered like diamonds. Of his antagonist I had only a back view, but that was sufficient I should not have cared to see his face.

He was apparently not more than fi e feet in height, with proportions suggesting those of a gorilla -- a tremendous breadth of shoulders, thick, short neck and broad, squat head, which had a tangled growth of black hair and was topped with a crimson fez. A tunic of the same colour, belted tightly to the waist, reached the seat -- apparently a box -- upon which he sat; his legs and feet were not seen. His left forearm appeared to rest in his lap; he moved his pieces with his right hand, which seemed disproportionately long.

I had shrunk back and now stood a little to one side of the doorway and in shadow. If Moxon had looked farther than the face of his opponent he could have observed nothing now, except that the door was open. Something forbade me either to enter or to retire, a feeling -- I know not how it came -- that I was in the presence of an imminent tragedy and might serve my friend by remaining. With a scarcely conscious rebellion against the indelicacy of the act, I remained.

The play was rapid. Moxon hardly glanced at the board before making his moves, and to my unskilled eye seemed to move the piece most convenient to his hand, his motions in doing so being quick, nervous, and lacking in precision. The response of his antagonist, while equally prompt in the inception, was made with a slow, uniform, mechanical and, I thought, somewhat theatrical movement of the arm that was a sore trial to my patience. There was something unearthly about it all, and I caught myself shuddering. But I

Exception - *Special/ Different from other*
Speculation - *Contemplation, Consideration*
Disproportion - *Unequal, Unsymmetical*
Imminent- *Likely to occur, Impending*
Antagonist - *Opponent, the opposite of a Hero in a story/ drama*

was wet and cold. Two or three times after moving a piece, the stranger slightly inclined his head, and each time I observed that Moxon shifted his king.

All at once the thought came to me that the man was dumb. And then that he was a machine -- an automaton chess player! Then I remembered that Moxon had once spoken to me of having invented such a piece of mechanism, though

I did not understand that it had actually been constructed. Was all his talk about the consciousness and intelligence of machines merely a prelude to eventual exhibition of this device -- only a trick to intensify the effect of its mechanical action upon me in my ignorance of its secret?

A fine end, this, of all my intellectual transports -- my 'endless variety and excitement of philosophic thought'! I was about to retire in disgust when something occurred to hold my curiosity.

I observed a shrug of the thing's great shoulders, as if it were irritated, and so natural was this -- so entirely human -- that in my new view of the matter it startled me. Nor was that all, for a moment later it struck the table sharply with its clenched hand. At that gesture Moxon seemed even more startled than I. He pushed his chair a little backward, as in alarm.

Presently Moxon, whose play it was, raised his hand high above the board, pounced upon one of his pieces like a sparrow-hawk and with the exclamation 'check-mate!' rose quickly to his feet and stepped behind his chair. The automaton sat motionless.

The wind had now gone down, but I heard, at lessening intervals and progressively louder, the rumble and roll of thunder. In the pauses between I now became conscious of a low humming or buzzing which, like the thunder, grew momentarily louder and more distinct.

It seemed to come from the body of the automaton, and was unmistakably a whirring of wheels. It gave me the impression of a disordered mechanism which had escaped the repressive and regulating action of some controlling part -- an effect such as might be expected if a pawl should be jostled from the teeth of a ratchetwheel. But before I had time for

Shuddering -
Trembling
Intensify -
Strengthen, Deepen
Prelude -
Introduction
Whirring -
Revolving/Moving with a buzzing sound

much conjecture as to its nature, my attention as taken by the strange motions of the automaton itself.

A slight but continuous convulsion appeared to have possession of it. In body and head it shook like a man with palsy or an ague chill, and the motion augmented every moment until the entire figure was in violent agitation. Suddenly it sprang to its feet and with a movement almost too quick for the eye to follow shot forward across table and chair, with both arms thrust forth to their full length -- the posture and lunge of a diver. Moxon tried to throw himself backward out of reach, but he was too late.

I saw the horrible thing's hand close upon his throat, his own clutch its wrists. Then the table was overturned, and candle thrown to the floor and extinguished, and all was black dark. But the noise of the struggle was dreadfully distinct, and most terrible of all were the raucous, squawking sounds made by the strangled man's efforts to breathe.

Guided by the infernal hubbub, I sprang to the rescue of my friend, but had hardly taken a stride in the darkness when the whole room blazed with a blinding white light that burned into my brain and heart and memory a vivid picture of the combatants on the floor, Moxon underneath, his throat still in the clutch of those iron hands, his head forced backward, his eyes protruding, his mouth wide open and his tongue thrust out; and -- horrible contrast! -- upon the painted face of his assassin an expression of tranquil and profound thought, as in the solution of a problem in chess! This I observed, then all was blackness and silence.

Three days later I recovered consciousness in a hospital. As the memory of that tragic night slowly evolved in my ailing brain I recognized in my attendant Moxon's confide - tial workman, Haley. Responding to a look he approached, smiling.

'Tell me about it,' I managed to say, faintly -- 'all about it.'

'Certainly,' he said; 'you were carried unconscious from a burning house -- Moxon's. Nobody knows how you came to be there. You may have to do a little explaining. The origin of the fire is a bit mysterious, too. My own notion is that the house was struck by lightning.'

'And Moxon?'

'Buried yesterday -- what was left of him.'

Infernal - *Devilish*
Hubbub - *A loud, confused noise*
Conjecture - *An opinion/theory*
Augmental - *To make larger in size, strength, number, etc.*

Apparently this reticent person could unfold himself on occasion. When imparting shocking intelligence to the sick, he was affable enough. After some moments of the keenest mental suffering I ventured to ask another question,

'Who rescued me?'

'Well, if that interests you -- I did.'

'Thank you, Mr. Haley, and may God bless you for it. Did you rescue, also, that charming product of your skill, the automaton chess player that murdered its inventor?'

The man was silent a long time, looking away from me. Presently he turned and gravely said,

'Do you know that?'

'I do,' I replied; 'I saw it done.'

That was many years ago. If asked today I should answer less confidently

Food For Thought

Why do you think the narrator in the story question at the end that whatever he saw was real or not? Moxon wins the game of chess but the automaton kills him after losing the game in anger. What does this signify and indicate?

Affable - *Cordial*
Automation - *Robot*
Apparently - *Evidently*
Ventured - *To undertake, Embark*

One Summer Night
~ Ambrose Bierce

The fact that Henry Armstrong was buried did not seem to him to prove that he was dead: he had always been a hard man to convince. That he really was buried, the testimony of his senses *compelled* him to admit. His posture -- flat upon his back, with his hands crossed upon his stomach and tied with something that he easily broke without profitably altering the situation -- the strict confinement of his entire person, the black darkness and *profound* silence, made a body of evidence impossible to *controvert* and he accepted it without *cavil*.

But dead -- no; he was only very, very ill. He had, *withal*, the invalid's apathy and did not greatly concern himself about the uncommon fate that had been allotted to him. No philosopher was he -- just a plain, commonplace person gifted, for the time being, with a pathological *indifferenc* : the organ that he feared consequences with was torpid. So, with no particular *apprehension* for his immediate future, he fell asleep and all was peace with Henry Armstrong.

But something was going on overhead. It was a dark summer night, shot through with infrequent shimmers of lightning silently firing a cloud lying low in the west and *portending* a storm. These brief, *stammering* illuminations brought out with ghastly distinctness the monuments and headstones of the cemetery and seemed to set them dancing. It was not a night in which any credible witness was likely to be straying about a cemetery, so the three men who were there, digging into the grave of Henry Armstrong, felt reasonably secure.

Two of them were young students from a medical college a few miles away; the third was a gigantic negro known as Jess. For many years, Jess had been employed about the cemetery as a man-of-all-work and it was his favourite pleasantry that he knew 'every soul in the place.' From the nature of what he was now doing it was *inferable* that the place was not so populous as its register may have shown it to be.

Outside the wall, at the part of the grounds farthest from the public road, were a horse and a light wagon, waiting.

The work of *excavation* was not difficult the earth with which the grave had been loosely filled a few hours before

Torpid - *Inactive*
Withal - *Inspited of all*
Cavil - *A trivila objection*
Controvert - *To aruge*
Inferable - *To guess*

offered little resistance and was soon thrown out. Removal of the *casket* from its box was less easy, but it was taken out, for it was a perquisite of Jess, who carefully unscrewed the cover and laid it aside, exposing the body in black trousers and white shirt. At that instant, the air sprang to flame, a cracking shock of thunder shook the stunned world and Henry Armstrong *tranquilly* sat up. With *inarticulate* cries, the men fled in terror, each in a different direction. For nothing on earth could two of them have been persuaded to return. But Jess was of another breed.

In the grey of the morning, the two students, *pallid* and *haggard* from anxiety and with the terror of their adventure still beating *tumultuously* in their blood, met at the medical college.

'You saw it?' cried one.

'God! yes -- what are we to do?'

They went around to the rear of the building, where they saw a horse, attached to a light wagon, *hitched* to a *gatepost* near the door of the dissecting-room. Mechanically they entered the room. On a bench in the *obscurity* sat the negro Jess. He rose, grinning, all eyes and teeth.

'I'm waiting for my pay,' he said.

Stretched naked on a long table lay the body of Henry Armstrong, the head *defile* with blood and clay from a blow with a spade.

Food For Thought

" I'm waiting for my pay." Who said this and why? What kind of pay was the speaker expecting from the two young students from a medical college?

Inarticulate - *Lacking the ability to express oneself*
Casket - *A coffin*
Haggard - *Wild*
Tumultuously - *Highly agrtated*
Obscurity - *Uncertainty*

My Favourite Murder
~ Ambrose Bierce

HAving murdered my mother under circumstances of singular atrocity, I was arrested and put upon my trial, which lasted seven years. In charging the jury, the judge of the Court of *Acquitta* remarked that it was one of the most ghastly crimes that he had ever been called upon to explain away.

At this, my attorney rose and said:

"May it please your Honour, crimes are ghastly or agreeable only by comparison. If you were familiar with the details of my client's previous murder of his uncle you would discern in his later offence (if offence it may be called) something in the nature of tender forbearance and *filia* consideration for the feelings of the victim. The *appalling ferocity* of the former assassination was indeed *inconsistent* with any hypothesis but that of guilt; and had it not been for the fact that the honourable judge before whom he was tried was the president of a life insurance company that took risks on hanging, and in which my client held a policy, it is hard to see how he could decently have been acquitted. If your Honour would like to hear about it for instruction and guidance of your Honour's mind, this unfortunate man, my client, will consent to give himself the pain of relating it under oath."

The district *attorne* said: "Your Honour, I object. Such a statement would be in the nature of evidence, and the testimony in this case is closed. The prisoner's statement should have been introduced three years ago, in the spring of 1881."

"In a statutory sense," said the judge, "you are right, and in the Court of Objections and Technicalities you would get a ruling in your favor. But not in a Court of *Acquitta*. The objection is overruled."

"I except," said the district attorney.

"You cannot do that," the judge said. "I must remind you that in order to take an *exception* you must first get this case transferred for a time to the Court of Exceptions on a formal motion duly supported by *affidavi*. A motion to that effect by your *predecessor* in offic was denied by me during the first ear of this trial. Mr. Clerk, swear the prisoner."

Filial - *Pertaining to*
Appaling - *To fill*
Acquittal - *Discharge*
Exceptions - *Something excepted*
Predecessor - *Succeeds*

The customary oath having been administered, I made the following statement, which *impressed* the judge with so strong a sense of the comparative triviality of the offence for which I was on trial that he made no further search for mitigating circumstances, but simply instructed the jury to acquit, and I left the court, without a stain upon my reputation:

"I was born in 1856 in Kalamakee, Mich., of honest and *reputable* parents, one of whom Heaven has mercifully spared to comfort me in my later years. In 1867 the family came to California and settled near Nigger Head, where my father opened a road agency and prospered beyond the dreams of avarice. He was a reticent, saturnine man then, though his increasing years have now somewhat relaxed the austerity of his disposition, and I believe that nothing but his memory of the sad event for which I am now on trial prevents him from manifesting a genuine *hilarity*.

"Four years after we had set up the road agency an *itinerant* preacher came along, and having no other way to pay for the night's lodging that we gave him, favored us with an exhortation of such power that, praise God, we were all converted to religion. My father at once sent for his brother the Hon. William Ridley of Stockton, and on his arrival turned over the agency to him, charging him nothing for the franchise nor plant - the latter consisting of a Winchester rifle, a sawed-off shotgun, and an *assortment* of masks made out of flour sacks. The family then moved to Ghost Rock and opened a dance house. It was called 'The Saints' Rest Hurdy-Gurdy,' and the proceedings each night began with prayer. It was there that my now sainted mother, by her grace in the dance, acquired the *sobriquet* of 'The Bucking Walrus.'

"In the fall of '75 I had occasion to visit Coyote, on the road to Mahala, and took the stage at Ghost Rock. There were four other passengers. About three miles beyond Nigger Head, persons whom I identified as my Uncle William and his two sons held up the stage. Finding nothing in the express box, they went through the passengers. I acted a most honourable part in the affair, placing myself in line with the others, holding up my hands and permitting myself to be *deprived* of forty dollars and a gold watch. From my behavior no one could have suspected that I knew the gentlemen who gave the entertainment. A few days later, when I went to Nigger Head and asked for the return of my money and watch my

Impressed - *Fascinated*
Reputable - *Honorarily*
Hilarity - *Cheerfulness*
Itinerant - *Travelling form place to place*
Assortment - *A collection*
Sobriquet - *Nickname*

uncle and cousins swore they knew nothing of the matt r, and they affected a belief that my father and I had done the job ourselves in dishonest violation of commercial good faith. Uncle William even threatened to *retaliate* by starting an opposition dance house at Ghost Rock. As 'The Saints' Rest' had become rather unpopular, I saw that this would assuredly ruin it and prove a paying enterprise, so I told my uncle that I was willing to overlook the past if he would take me into the scheme and keep the partnership a secret from my father. This fair offer he rejected, and I then perceived that it would be better and more satisfactory if he ere dead.

"My plans to that end were soon perfected, and communicating them to my dear parents I had the *gratificatio* of receiving their approval. My father said he was proud of me, and my mother promised that although her religion forbade her to assist in taking human life I should have the advantage of her prayers for my success. As a preliminary measure looking to my security in case of *detection* I made an application for membership in that powerful order, the Knights of Murder, and in due course was received as a member of the Ghost Rock *commandery*. On the day that my probation ended I was for the first time permitted to inspect the records of the order and learn who belonged to it - all the rites of initiation having been conducted in masks. Fancy my delight when, in looking over the roll of membership, I found the third name to be that of my uncle, who indeed was junior vice-chancellor of the order! Here was an opportunity exceeding my wildest dreams - to murder I could add insubordination and treachery. It was what my good mother would have called 'a special Providence.'

"At about this time something occurred which caused my cup of joy, already full, to overflow on all sides, a circular cataract of bliss. Three men, strangers in that locality, were arrested for the stage robbery in which I had lost my money and watch. They were brought to trial and, despite my effort to clear them and fasten the guilt upon three of the most respectable and worthy citizens of Ghost Rock, convicted on the clearest proof. The murder would now be as wanton and reasonless as I could wish.

"One morning I shouldered my Winchester rifle, and going over to my uncle's house, near Nigger Head, asked my Aunt Mary, his wife, if he were at home, adding that I had

Retaliate - *To reciprocate, repay*
Gratifi ation - *Great satisfaction*
Detection - *The act of discovering*
Commandery - *Th offi*

come to kill him. My aunt replied with her peculiar smile that so many gentleman called on that *errand* and were afterward carried away without having performed it that I must excuse her for doubting my good faith in the matter. She said I did not look as if I would kill anybody, so, as a proof of good faith I levelled my rifle and wounded a Chinaman who happened to be passing the house. She said she knew whole families that could do a thing of that kind, but Bill Ridley was a horse of another colour. She said, however, that I would find him over on the other side of the *creek* in the sheep lot; and she added that she hoped the best man would win.

"My Aunt Mary was one of the most fair-minded women that I have ever met.

"I found my uncle down on his knees engaged in skinning a sheep. Seeing that he had neither gun nor pistol handy I had not the heart to shoot him, so I approached him, greeted him pleasantly and struck him a powerful blow on the head with the butt of my rifle. I have a very good delivery and Uncle William lay down on his side, then rolled over on his back, spread out his fingers and shivered. Before he could recover the use of his limbs I seized the knife that he had been using and cut his hamstrings. You know, doubtless, that when you sever the Achilles tendon, the patient has no further use of his leg; it is just the same as if he had no leg. Well, I parted them both, and when he *revived* he was at my service. As soon as he *comprehended* the situation, he said:

" 'Samuel, you have got the drop on me and can afford to be generous. I have only one thing to ask of you, and that is that you carry me to the house and finish me in the bosom of my family.'

"I told him I thought that a pretty reasonable request and I would do so if he would let me put him into a wheat sack; he would be easier to carry that way and if we were seen by the neighbours en route it would cause less remark. He agreed to that, and going to the barn I got a sack. This, however, did not fit him; it was too short and much wider than he; so I bent his legs, forced his knees up against his breast and got him into it that way, tying the sack above his head. He was a heavy man and I had all that I could do to get him on my back, but I *staggered* along for some distance until I came to a swing that some of the children had suspended to the branch of an oak. Here I laid him down and sat upon him to rest, and the sight

---

Errand - *A short and quick trip*
Creek - *A stream*
Comprehended - *Perceived*
Staggered - *To walk/move*
Revived - *To restore to life, vigour*

of the rope gave me a happy inspiration. In twenty minutes my uncle, still in the sack, swung free to the sport of the wind.

"I had taken down the rope, tied one end tightly about the mouth of the bag, thrown the other across the limb and *hauled* him up about fi e feet from the ground. Fastening the other end of the rope also about the mouth of the sack, I had the satisfaction to see my uncle converted into a large, fine pendulum. I must add that he was not himself entirely aware of the nature of the change that he had undergone in his relation to the exterior world, though in justice to a good man's memory I ought to say that I do not think he would in any case have wasted much of my time in vain *remonstrance*.

"Uncle William had a ram that was famous in all that region as a fighter. It was in a state of chronic constitutional indignation. Some deep disappointment in early life had soured its disposition and it had declared war upon the whole world. To say that it would butt anything accessible is but faintly to express the nature and scope of its military activity: the universe was its antagonist; its methods that of a projectile. It fought like the angels and devils, in mid-air, cleaving the atmosphere like a bird, describing a *parabolic* curve and descending upon its victim at just the exact angle of incidence to make the most of its velocity and weight. Its momentum, calculated in foot-tons, was something incredible. It had been seen to destroy a four year old bull by a single impact upon that animal's gnarly forehead. No stone wall had ever been known to resist its downward swoop; there were no trees tough enough to stay it; it would splinter them into matchwood and defile their leafy honours in the dust. This *irascible* and *implacable* brute - this *incarnate* thunderbolt - this monster of the upper deep, I had seen reposing in the shade of an adjacent tree, dreaming dreams of conquest and glory. It was with a view to summoning it forth to the field of honour that I suspended its master in the manner described.

"Having completed my preparations, I imparted to the *avuncular* pendulum a gentle oscillation, and retiring to cover behind a contiguous rock, lifted up my voice in a long rasping cry whose diminishing final note was drowned in a noise like that of a swearing cat, which *emanated* from the sack. Instantly that *formidable* sheep was upon its feet and had taken in the military situation at a glance. In a few moments it had approached, stamping, to within fifty yards of the swinging foeman, who, now retreating and anon advancing, seemed to invite

Hauled - *To pull/ draw with force*
Remonstrance - *A protest*
Parabolic - *Pertaining to*
Incarnate - *Personifi d*
Implacable - *Unappeasable*
Avuncular - *Resembling an uncle*
Formidable - *Powerfull, of great strength*

the fray. Suddenly I saw the beast's head drop earthward as if depressed by the weight of its enormous horns; then a dim, white, wavy streak of sheep prolonged itself from that spot in a generally horizontal direction to within about four yards of a point immediately beneath the enemy. There it struck sharply upward, and before it had faded from my gaze at the place whence it had set out I heard a horrid thump and a piercing scream, and my poor uncle shot forward, with a slack rope higher than the limb to which he was attached. Here the rope tautened with a jerk, arresting his flight, and back he swung in a breathless curve to the other end of his arc. The ram had fallen, a heap of indistinguishable legs, wool and horns, but pulling itself together and dodging as its antagonist swept downward it retired at random, alternately shaking its head and stamping its fore-feet. When it had backed about the same distance as that from which it had delivered the assault it paused again, bowed its head as if in prayer for victory and again shot forward, dimly visible as before - a prolonging white streak with monstrous undulations, ending with a sharp ascension. Its course this time was at a right angle to its former one, and its impatience so great that it struck the enemy before he had nearly reached the lowest point of his arc. In consequence he went flying round and round in a horizontal circle whose radius was about equal to half the length of the rope, which I forgot to say was nearly twenty feet long. His shrieks, crescendo in approach and diminuendo in recession, made the rapidity of his revolution more obvious to the ear than to the eye. He had evidently not yet been struck in a vital spot. His posture in the sack and the distance from the ground at which he hung compelled the ram to operate upon his lower extremities and the end of his back. Like a plant that has struck its root into some poisonous mineral, my poor uncle was dying slowly upward.

"After delivering its second blow the ram had not again retired. The fever of battle burned hot in its heart; its brain was intoxicated with the wine of strife. Like a pugilist who in his rage forgets his skill and fights ineffecti ely at half-arm's length, the angry beast endeavored to reach its fleeting foe by awkward vertical leaps as he passed overhead, sometimes, indeed, succeeding in striking him feebly, but more frequently overthrown by its own misguided eagerness. But as the impetus was exhausted and the man's circles narrowed in scope and diminished in speed, bringing him nearer to the ground, these tactics produced better

Antagonist -
Opponent
Diminuendo -
Gradually reducing in force
Compelled - *Forced*
Pugilist - *Boxer*
Endeavoured -
Ventured
Tactics - *Plan*

results, eliciting a superior quality of screams, which I greatly enjoyed.

"Suddenly, as if the bugles had sung truce, the ram suspended hostilities and walked away, thoughtfully wrinkling and smoothing its great aquiline nose, and occasionally cropping a bunch of grass and slowly munching it. It seemed to have tired of war's alarms and resolved to beat the sword into a plowshare and cultivate the arts of peace. Steadily it held its course away from the field of fame until it had gained a distance of nearly a quarter of a mile. There it stopped and stood with its rear to the foe, chewing its cud and apparently half asleep. I observed, however, an occasional slight turn of its head, as if its apathy were more affected than real.

"Meantime Uncle William's shrieks had abated with his motion, and nothing was heard from him but long, low moans, and at long intervals my name, uttered in pleading tones exceedingly grateful to my ear. Evidently the man had not the faintest notion of what was being done to him, and was inexpressibly terrified. When Death comes cloaked in mystery he is terrible indeed. Little by little my uncle's oscillations diminished, and finally, he hung motionless. I went to him and was about to give him the coup de grace, when I heard and felt a succession of smart shocks which shook the ground like a series of light earthquakes, and turning in the direction of the ram, saw a long cloud of dust approaching me with inconceivable rapidity and alarming effect! At a distance of some thirty yards away it stopped short, and from the near end of it rose into the air what I at first thought a great white bird. Its ascent was so smooth and easy and regular that I could not realize its extraordinary celerity, and was lost in admiration of its grace. To this day the impression remains that it was a slow, deliberate movement, the ram - for it was that animal - being upborne by some power other than its own impetus, and supported through the successive stages of its flight with infinite tenderness and care. My eyes followed its progress through the air with unspeakable pleasure, all the greater by contrast with my former terror of its approach by land. Onward and upward the noble animal sailed, its head bent down almost between its knees, its fore-feet thrown back, its hinder legs trailing to rear like the legs of a soaring heron.

"At a height of forty or fifty feet, as fond recollection pre-ents it to view, it attained its *zenith* and appeared to remain an instant stationary; then, tilting suddenly forward without

Bugies - *Bugle*
Truce - *Peace*
Aquiline - *Shaped like an eagle*
Cud - *Beak*
Inconceivable - *Unbelievable*
Celerity - *Swift ess*

altering the relative position of its parts, it shot downward on a steeper and steeper course with augmenting velocity, passed immediately above me with a noise like the rush of a cannon shot and struck my poor uncle almost squarely on the top of the head! So frightful was the impact that not only the man's neck was broken, but the rope too; and the body of the **deceased**, forced against the earth, was crushed to pulp beneath the awful front of that meteoric sheep! The concussion stopped all the clocks between Lone Hand and Dutch Dan's, and Professor Davidson, a distinguished authority in matters **seismic**, who happened to be in the vicinity, promptly explained that the vibrations were from north to southwest.

"Altogether, I cannot help thinking that in point of artistic **atrocity** my murder of Uncle William has seldom been excelled."

Deceased - *No longer living, dead*
Atrocity - *Cruelty*
Seismic - *Relating to*

Food For Thought

How do you like this story? Do you feel that the story is humorous or a serious one? How do you like the ending of the story? Can you suggest some other possible ending to the story?

John Mortonson's Funeral
~ Ambrose Bierce

JOhn Mortonson was dead: his lines in 'the tragedy "Man"' had all been spoken and he had left the stage.

The body rested in a fine *mahogany* coffi fitte with a plate of glass. All arrangements for the *funeral* had been so well attended to that had the *deceased* known he would doubtless have *approved*. The face, as it showed under the glass, was not *disagreeable* to look upon: it bore a faint smile, and as the death had been painless, had not been *distorted* beyond the repairing power of the undertaker. At two o'clock of the afternoon the friends were to assemble to pay their last tribute of respect to one who had no further need of friends and respect. The surviving members of the family came severally every few minutes to the *casket* and wept above the placid features beneath the glass. This did them no good; it did no good to John Mortonson; but in the presence of death reason and philosophy are silent.

As the hour of two approached, the friends began to arrive and after offering such *consolation* to the stricken relatives as the *proprieties* of the occasion required, solemnly seated themselves about the room with an *augmented* consciousness of their importance in the scheme funereal. Then the minister came, and in that overshadowing presence the lesser lights went into eclipse. His entrance was followed by that of the widow, whose *lamentations* filled the room. She approached the casket and after leaning her face against the cold glass for a moment was gently led to a seat near her daughter. Mournfully and low the man of God began his *eulogy* of the dead, and his doleful voice, mingled with the *sobbing* which it was its purpose to stimulate and sustain, rose and fell, seemed to come and go, like the sound of a sullen sea. The gloomy day grew darker as he spoke; a curtain of cloud underspread the sky and a few drops of rain fell audibly. It seemed as if all nature were weeping for John Mortonson.

When the minister had finished his eulogy with prayer a hymn was sung and the *pall-bearers* took their places beside the bier. As the last notes of the hymn died away the widow ran to the coffin cast herself upon it and sobbed *hysterically*.

Hysterically - *Uncontrollably emotional*
Casket - *A small chest*
Lamentation - *Expressing grief*
Eulogy - *A speech writing in praise*
Proprieties - *Decency, modesty*
Avgmented - *Enlarge in size*

Gradually, however, she *yielded* to *dissuasion*, becoming more *composed*; and as the minister was in the act of leading her away, her eyes sought the face of the dead beneath the glass. She threw up her arms and with a *shriek* fell backward insensible.

The *mourners* sprang forward to the coffin the friends followed, and as the clock on the *mantel solemnly* struck three, all were staring down upon the face of John Mortonson, deceased. They turned away, sick and faint. One man, trying in his terror to escape the awful sight, *stumbled* against the coffi so heavily as to knock away one of its frail supports. The coffi fell to the floor, the glass was shattered to bits by the *concussion*.

From the opening crawled John Mortonson's cat, which lazily leapt to the floor, sat up, *tranquilly* wiped its crimson muzzle with a forepaw, then walked with dignity from the room.

Food For Thought

John Mortonson's cat had pounced his paws and drank the blood of his own master. What sort of sight do you think it would have been? Why did the cat attack his own master? Do such things happen and have you ever come across any such incident in your life?

Yielded - *To produce, give up*
Dissuasion - *To advise against*
Mourners - *Persons who attend a funeral of a deceased*
Mantel - *A construction of a fi eplace*
Concussion - *Injury to the brain*
Tranquilly - *Peacefully*

John Bartine's Watch
~ Ambrose Bierce

A Story by a Physician

'The exact time? Good God! My friend, why do you **insist**? One would think -- but what does it matter; it is easily bedtime -- isn't that near enough? But, here, if you must set your watch, take mine and see for yourself.'

With that he **detached** his watch -- a **tremendously** heavy, old-fashioned one -- from the chain, and handed it to me; then turned away, and walking across the room to a shelf of books, began an examination of their backs. His **agitation** and evident **distress** surprised me; they appeared reasonless. Having set my watch by his I stepped over to where he stood and said, 'Thank you.'

As he took his timepiece and reattached it to the guard I observed that his hands were unsteady. With a tact upon which I greatly prided myself, I **sauntered** carelessly to the sideboard and took some brandy and water; then, begging his pardon for my thoughtlessness, asked him to have some and went back to my seat by the fire, leaving him to help himself, as was our custom. He did so and presently joined me at the hearth, as **tranquil** as ever.

This odd little incident occurred in my apartment, where John Bartine was passing an evening. We had dined together at the club, had come home in a cab and -- in short, everything had been done in the most **prosaic** way; and why John Bartine should break in upon the natural and established order of things to make himself **spectacular** with a display of emotion, apparently for his own entertainment, I could nowise understand. The more I thought of it, while his brilliant conversational gifts were commending themselves to my inattention, the more curious I grew, and of course had no difficult in persuading myself that my curiosity was friendly **solicitude**. That is the disguise that curiosity usually assumes to evade **resentment**. So I ruined one of the finest sentences of his disregarded monologue by cutting it short without ceremony

'John Bartine,' I said, 'you must try to forgive me if I am wrong, but with the light that I have at present I cannot **concede** your right to go all to pieces when asked the time o' night.

Detach – Separate
Saunter – Stroll
Prosaic – Dull
Tranquil – Calm

I cannot admit that it is proper to experience a mysterious reluctance to look your own watch in the face and to *cherish* in my presence, without explanation, painful emotions which are denied to me, and which are none of my business.'

To this ridiculous speech Bartine made no immediate reply, but sat looking gravely into the fire. Fearing that I had *offended* I was about to apologize and beg him to think no more about the matter, when looking me calmly in the e es he said,

'My dear fellow, the *levity* of your manner does not at all disguise the hideous *impudence* of your demand; but happily I had already decided to tell you what you wish to know, and no manifestation of your unworthiness to hear it shall alter my decision. Be good enough to give me your attention and you shall hear all about the matter

'This watch,' he said, 'had been in my family for three generations before it fell to me. Its original owner, for whom it was made, was my great-grandfather, Bramwell Olcott Bartine, a wealthy planter of Colonial Virginia, and as *staunch* a Tory as ever lay awake nights contriving new kinds of maledictions for the head of Mr. Washington, and new methods of aiding and *abettin* good King George. One day this worthy gentleman had the deep misfortune to perform for his cause a service of capital importance which was not recognized as legitimate by those who suffered its disadvantages. It does not matter what it was, but among its minor consequences was my excellent ancestor's arrest one night in his own house by a party of Mr. Washington's rebels. He was permitted to say farewell to his weeping family, and was then marched away into the darkness which swallowed him up for ever. Not the slenderest clue to his fate was ever found. After the war the most diligent inquiry and the offer of large rewards failed to turn up any of his captors or any fact concerning his disappearance. He had disappeared, and that was all.'

Something in Bartine's manner that was not in his words -- I hardly knew what it was -- prompted me to ask,

'What is your view of the matter -- of the justice of it?

'My view of it,' he flamed out, bringing his clenched hand down upon the table as if he had been in a public house dicing with blackguards -- 'my view of it is that it was a characteristically dastardly assassination by that damned *traitor*, Washington, and his *ragamuffin* rebels!'

Levity – Lightness
Impudence – Nerve
Abetti g – Encouraging
Traitor - *A person who betrays another*
Ragamuffin – Ragged, Disreputable persons

For some minutes nothing was said, Bartine was recovering his temper, and I waited. Then I said,

'Was that all?'

'No -- there was something else. A few weeks after my great-grandfather's arrest, his watch was found lying on the porch at the front door of his *dwelling*. It was wrapped in a sheet of letter-paper bearing the name of Rupert Bartine, his only son, my grandfather. I am wearing that watch.'

Bartine paused. His usually restless black eyes were staring fixedly into the grate, a point of red light in each, reflected from the glowing coals. He seemed to have forgotten me. A sudden *threshing* of the branches of a tree outside one of the windows, and almost at the same instant a rattle of rain against the glass, recalled him to a sense of his surroundings. A storm had risen, heralded by a single gust of wind, and in a few moments the steady plash of the water on the pavement was distinctly heard. I hardly know why I relate this incident; it seemed somehow to have a certain significance and relevancy which I am unable now to *discern*. It at least added an element of seriousness, almost **solemnity**. Bartine resumed,

'I have a singular feeling toward this watch -- a kind of affection for it; I like to have it about me, though partly from its weight, and partly for a reason I shall now explain, I seldom carry it. The reason is this: Every evening when I have it with me I feel an unaccountable desire to open and consult it, even if I can think of no reason for wishing to know the time. But if I *yield* to it, the moment my eyes rest upon the dial I am filled with a mysterious *apprehension* -- a sense of imminent calamity. And this is the more insupportable the nearer it is to eleven o'clock -- by this watch, no matter what the actual hour may be. After the hands have registered eleven the desire to look is gone; I am entirely indifferent. Then I can consult the thing as often as I like, with no more emotion than you feel in looking at your own. Naturally I have trained myself not to look at that watch in the evening before eleven; nothing could *induce* me. Your insistence this evening upset me a trifle. I felt very much as I suppose an opium-eater might feel if his yearning for his special and particular kind of hell were reinforced by opportunity and advice.

'Now that is my story, and I have told it in the interest of your *trumpery* science; but if on any evening hereafter you observe me wearing this damnable watch, and you have the

Th eshing – *Thrash*
Discern – *Discriminate*
Apprehension – *Worry*
Induce – *Encourage*

thoughtfulness to ask me the hour, I shall beg leave to put you to the inconvenience of being knocked down.'

His humour did not *amuse* me. I could see that in relating his *delusion* he was again somewhat disturbed. His concluding smile was positively ghastly, and his eyes had resumed something more than their old restlessness; they shifted hither and thither about the room with apparent aimlessness and I fancied had taken on a wild expression, such as is sometimes observed in cases of dementia. Perhaps this was my own imagination, but at any rate I was now persuaded that my friend was afflicte with a most singular and interesting monomania. Without, I trust, any *abatement* of my affectio - ate solicitude for him as a friend, I began to regard him as a patient, rich in possibilities of profitable study. Why not? Had he not described his delusion in the interest of science? Ah, poor fellow, he was doing more for science than he knew: not only his story but himself was in evidence. I should cure him if I could, of course, but first I should make a little experiment in psychology -- nay, the experiment itself might be a step in his *restoration*.

'That is very frank and friendly of you, Bartine,' I said cordially, 'and I'm rather proud of your confidence. It is all very odd, certainly. Do you mind showing me the watch?'

He detached it from his waistcoat, chain and all, and passed it to me without a word. The case was of gold, very thick and strong, and singularly *engraved*. After closely examining the dial and observing that it was nearly twelve o'clock, I opened it at the back and was interested to observe an inner case of ivory, upon which was painted a miniature portrait in that exquisite and delicate manner which was in vogue during the eighteenth century.

'Why, bless my soul!' I exclaimed, feeling a sharp artistic *delight* -- 'how under the sun did you get that done? I thought *miniature* painting on ivory was a lost art.'

'That,' he replied, gravely smiling, 'is not I; it is my excellent great-grandfather, the late Bramwell Olcott Bartine, Esquire, of Virginia. He was younger then than later -- about my age, in fact. It is said to *resemble* me; do you think so?'

'Resemble you? I should say so! Barring the costume, which I supposed you to have assumed out of compliment to the art -- or for vraisemblance, so to say -- and the no moustache, that portrait is you in every feature, line, and expression.'

Dementia – *Madness*
Monomania – *Obsession*
Vogue – *Trend*
Miniature – *Small*

No more was said at that time. Bartine took a book from the table and began reading. I heard outside the *incessant* plash of the rain in the street. There were occasional hurried footfalls on the sidewalks; and once a slower, heavier *tread* seemed to cease at my door -- a policeman, I thought, seeking shelter in the doorway. The boughs of the trees tapped significantly on the window panes, as if asking for admittance. I remember it all through these years and years of a wiser, graver life.

Seeing myself unobserved, I took the old-fashioned key that dangled from the chain and quickly turned back the hands of the watch a full hour; then, closing the case, I handed Bartine his property and saw him replace it on his person.

'I think you said,' I began, with assumed carelessness, 'that after eleven the sight of the dial no longer affects you. As it is now nearly twelve' -- looking at my own timepiece -- 'perhaps, if you don't resent my pursuit of proof, you will look at it now.'

He smiled good humouredly, pulled out the watch again, opened it, and instantly sprang to his feet with a cry that Heaven has not had the mercy to permit me to forget! His eyes, their blackness strikingly intensified by the *pallor* of his face, were fixed upon the watch, which he clutched in both hands. For some time he remained in that attitude without uttering another sound; then, in a voice that I should not have recognized as his, he said,

'Damn you! It is two minutes to eleven!'

I was not unprepared for some such *outbreak*, and without rising replied, calmly enough,

'I beg your pardon; I must have misread your watch in setting my own by it.'

He shut the case with a sharp snap and put the watch in his pocket. He looked at me and made an attempt to smile, but his lower lip quivered and he seemed unable to close his mouth. His hands, also, were shaking, and he thrust them, clenched, into the pockets of his sack coat. The courageous spirit was manifestly endeavouring to subdue the coward body. The effort was too great; he began to sway from side to side, as from vertigo, and before I could spring from my chair to support him his knees gave way and he pitched awkwardly forward and fell upon his face. I sprang to assist him to rise; but when John Bartine rises we shall all rise.

Incessant – *Nonstop*
Pallor – *Whiteness*
Endeavour – *Attempt*
Vertigo – *Dizziness*

The post-mortem examination disclosed nothing; every organ was normal and sound. But when the body had been prepared for burial a faint dark circle was seen to have developed around the neck; at least I was so assured by several persons who said they saw it, but of my own knowledge I cannot say if that was true.

Nor can I set limitations to the law of **heredity**. I do not know that in the spiritual world a *sentiment* or emotion may not survive the heart that held it, and seek expression in a **kindred** life, ages removed. Surely, if I were to guess at the fate of Bramwell Olcott Bartine, I should guess that he was hanged at eleven o'clock in the evening, and that he had been allowed several hours in which to prepare for the change.

As to John Bartine, my friend, my patient for fi e minutes, and -- Heaven forgive me! -- My *victim* for *eternity*, there is no more to say. He is buried, and his watch with him -- I saw to that. May God rest his soul in Paradise, and the soul of his Virginian *ancestor*, if, indeed, they are two souls.

Food For Thought

What happened at eleven in the night? Why did the narrator of the story feel that John Bartine's body was captured by the spirit of Bartine's great-grandfather? Do you think the narrator was right? How did Bartine die? Was it a normal death? Give reasons for your answer.

Viction – *A person who suffers harm*
Heredity – *Genetics*
Kindred – *Relatives*
Eternity – *Infinity*
Ancestor – *Rootage*

An Inhabitant Of Carcosa
- Ambrose Bierce

FOr there be divers sorts of death -- some wherein the body remaineth; and in some it vanisheth quite away with the spirit. This commonly occurreth only in **solitude** (such is God's will) and, none seeing the end, we say the man is lost, or gone on a long journey -- which indeed he hath; but sometimes it hath happened in sight of many, as **abundant testimony** showeth. In one kind of death the spirit also dieth, and this it hath been known to do while yet the body was in **vigour** for many years. Sometimes, as is **veritably atteste**, it dieth with the body, but after a season is raised up again in that place where the body did **decay**.

Pondering these words of Hali (whom God rest) and questioning their full meaning, as one who, having an **intimation**, yet doubts if there be not something behind, other than that which he has discerned, I noted not whither I had strayed until a sudden chill wind striking my face revived in me a sense of my surroundings. I observed with **astonishment** that everything seemed unfamiliar. On every side of me stretched a bleak and desolate expanse of plain, covered with a tall overgrowth of sere grass, which rustled and whistled in the autumn wind with Heaven knows what mysterious and **disquieting** suggestion. Protruded at long intervals above it, stood strangely shaped and somber-coloured rocks, which seemed to have an understanding with one another and to exchange looks of uncomfortable significance, as if they had reared their heads to watch the issue of some foreseen event. A few blasted trees here and there appeared as leaders in this **malevolent conspiracy** of silent expectation.

The day, I thought, must be far advanced, though the sun was invisible; and although sensible that the air was raw and chill my consciousness of that fact was rather mental than physical -- I had no feeling of discomfort. Over all the **dismal** landscape a canopy of low, lead-coloured clouds hung like a visible curse. In all this there was a **menace** and a **portent** -- a hint of evil, an intimation of **doom**. Bird, beast, or insect there was none. The wind sighed in the bare branches of the dead trees and the grey grass bent to whisper its dread secret to the

Testimony - *Proof*
Veritably - *In fact*
Discerned - *Anticipated*
Malevolent - *Wicked*

earth; but no other sound nor motion broke the awful repose of that dismal place.

I observed in the herbage a number of weatherworn stones, evidently shaped with tools. They were broken, covered with moss and half sunken in the earth. Some lay prostrate, some leaned at various angles, none was vertical. They were obviously headstones of graves, though the graves themselves no longer existed as either mounds or depressions; the years had levelled all. Scattered here and there, more massive blocks showed where some *pompous* tomb or ambitious monument had once flung its feeble defiance at oblivion. So old seemed these relics, these vestiges of vanity and memorials of affection and piety, so battered and worn and stained -- so neglected, deserted, forgotten the place, that I could not help thinking myself the discoverer of the burial ground of a prehistoric race of men whose very name was long extinct.

Filled with these reflections, I was for some time heedless of the sequence of my own experiences, but soon I thought, 'How came I hither?' A moment's reflection seemed to mak this all clear and explain at the same time, though in a disquieting way, the singular character with which my fancy had invested all that I saw or heard. I was ill. I remembered now that I had been prostrated by a sudden fever, and that my family had told me that in my periods of *delirium* I had constantly cried out for liberty and air, and had been held in bed to prevent my escape out-of-doors. Now I had eluded the *vigilance* of my attendants and had wandered hither to -- to where? I could not conjecture. Clearly I was at a considerable distance from the city where I dwelt -- the ancient and famous city of Carcosa.

No signs of human life were anywhere visible nor audible; no rising smoke, no watch-dog's bark, no lowing of cattle, no shouts of children at play--nothing but that dismal burial place, with its air of mystery and *dread*, due to my own disordered brain. Was I not becoming again delirious, there beyond human aid? Was it not indeed all an illusion of my madness? I called aloud the names of my wives and sons, reached out my hands in search of theirs, even as I walked among the crumbling stones and in the withered grass.

A noise behind me caused me to turn about. A wild animal -- a lynx -- was approaching. The thought came to me, if I break down here in the desert -- if the fever return and I fail, this

Repose – *Relax*
Evidently – *Clearly*
Pompous – *Arrogant*
Prostrated – *Surrender*

beast will be at my throat. I sprang toward it, shouting. It trotted tranquilly by within a hand's-breadth of me and disappeared behind a rock.

A moment later a man's head appeared to rise out of the ground a short distance away. He was ascending the farther slope of a low hill whose crest was hardly to be distinguished from the general level. His whole figure soon came into view against the background of grey cloud. He was half naked, half clad in skins. His hair was *unkempt*, his beard long and ragged. In one hand he carried a bow and arrow; the other held a blazing torch with a long trail of black smoke. He walked slowly and with caution, as if he feared falling into some open grave concealed by the tall grass. This strange apparition surprised but did not alarm, and taking such a course as to intercept him I met him almost face to face, accosting him with the familiar salutation, 'God keep you.'

He gave no heed, nor did he arrest his pace.

'Good stranger,' I continued, 'I am ill and lost. Direct me, I beseech you, to Carcosa.'

The man broke into a barbarous chant in an unknown tongue, passing on and away.

An owl on the branch of a *decayed* tree hooted dismally and was answered by another in the distance. Looking upward, I saw through a sudden rift in the clouds Aldebaran and the Hyades! In all this there was a hint of night -- the lynx, the man with the torch, the owl. Yet I saw -- I saw even the stars in absence of the darkness. I saw, but was apparently not seen nor heard. Under what *awful* spell did I exist?

I seated myself at the root of a great tree, seriously to consider what it were best to do. That I was mad I could no longer doubt, yet recognized a ground of doubt in the conviction. Of fever I had no trace. I had, withal, a sense of exhilaration and *vigour* altogether unknown to me -- a feeling of mental and physical exaltation. My senses seemed all alert; I could feel the air as a ponderous substance; I could hear the silence.

A great root of the giant tree against whose trunk I leaned as I sat held enclosed in its grasp a slab of stone, a part of which protruded into a recess formed by another root. The stone was thus partly protected from the weather, though greatly decomposed. Its edges were worn round, its corners eaten away,

Ascending – *Climbing*
Apparition – *Spirit*
Intercept – *Catch*
Beseech – *Ask*

its surface deeply furrowed and scaled. Glittering particles of mica were visible in the earth about it--vestiges of its decomposition. This stone had apparently marked the grave out of which the tree had sprung ages ago. The tree's exacting roots had robbed the grave and made the stone a prisoner.

A sudden wind pushed some dry leaves and twigs from the uppermost face of the stone; I saw the low relief letters of an inscription and bent to read it. God in heaven! My name in full! -- The date of my birth! -- The date of my death!

A level shaft of light illuminated the whole side of the tree as I sprang to my feet in terror. The sun was rising in the rosy east. I stood between the tree and his broad red disk -- no shadow darkened the trunk!

A chorus of howling wolves saluted the dawn. I saw them sitting on their haunches, singly and in groups, on the summits of irregular mounds and tumuli filling a half of my desert prospect and extending to the horizon. And then I knew that these were ruins of the ancient and famous city of Carcosa.

Such are the facts *imparted* to the medium Bayrolles by the spirit Hoseib Alar Robardin.

Food For Thought

What would you do if you suddenly remembered that you were a famous doctor or a philosopher in your previous birth? Write a few lines about it and your feelings as well as your behaviour that would change if something like this happens with you.

Inscription – *Writing on metal or wood*
Shaft – *Beam*
Illuminated – *Brightened*
Imparted – *Announced, communicated*

An Occurrence at Owl Creek Bridge

Ambrose Bierce

A man stood upon a railroad bridge in northern Alabama, looking down into the swift water twenty feet below. The man's hands were behind his back, the wrists bound with a cord. A rope closely encircled his neck. It was attached to a **stout** cross-timber above his head and the slack feel to the level of his knees. Some loose boards laid upon the ties supporting the rails of the railway supplied a footing for him and his executioners - two private soldiers of the Federal army, directed by a sergeant who in civil life may have been a deputy sheriff. At a short remove upon the same temporary platform was an office in the uniform of his rank, armed. He was a captain. A sentinel at each end of the bridge stood with his rifle in the position known as "support", that is to say, vertical in front of the left shoulder, the hammer resting on the forearm thrown straight across the chest - a formal and unnatural position, enforcing an erect carriage of the body. It did not appear to be the duty of these two men to know what was occurring at the center of the bridge; they merely blockaded the two ends of the foot planking that traversed it.

Beyond one of the sentinels nobody was in sight; the railroad ran straight away into a forest for a hundred yards, then, curving, was lost to view. Doubtless there was an outpost farther along. The other bank of the stream was open ground - a gentle slope topped with a stockade of vertical tree trunks, loop-holed for rifles, with a single **embrasure** through which **protruded** the muzzle of a brass cannon commanding the bridge. Midway up the slope between the bridge and fort were the spectators - a single company of infantry in line, at 'parade rest,' the butts of their rifles on the ground, the barrels inclining slightly backward against the right shoulder, the hands crossed upon the stock. A lieutenant stood at the right of the line, the point of his sword upon the ground, his left hand resting upon his right. Excepting the group of four at the center of the bridge, not a man moved. The company faced the bridge, staring stonily, motionless. The sentinels, facing

Stout – *Heavily built*
Executioners – *Offi als who inflict capital, punishment*
Blockaded – *Closure*
Embrasure – *Cavity*

the banks of the stream, might have been statues to *adorn* the bridge. The captain stood with folded arms, silent, observing the work of his subordinates, but making no sign. Death is a dignitary who when he comes announced is to be received with formal *manifestations* of respect, even by those most familiar with him. In the code of military *etiquett* silence and fixity are forms of deference

The man who was engaged in being hanged was apparently about thirty-fi e years of age. He was a civilian, if one might judge from his habit, which was that of a planter. His features were good - a straight nose, firm mouth, broad forehead, from which his long, dark hair was combed straight back, falling behind his ears to the collar of his well fi ing frock coat.

He wore a moustache and pointed beard, but no whiskers; his eyes were large and dark gray, and had a kindly expression which one would hardly have expected in one whose neck was in the hemp. Evidently this was no *vulgar assassin*. The liberal military code makes provision for hanging many kinds of persons, and gentlemen are not excluded.

The preparations being complete, the two private soldiers stepped aside and each drew away the plank upon which he had been standing. The sergeant turned to the captain, saluted and placed himself immediately behind that officer who in turn moved apart one pace. These movements left the *condemned* man and the sergeant standing on the two ends of the same plank, which spanned three of the cross-ties of the bridge. The end upon which the civilian stood almost, but not quite, reached a fourth. This plank had been held in place by the weight of the captain; it was now held by that of the sergeant.

At a signal from the former the *latte* would step aside, the plank would tilt and the condemned man go down between two ties. The arrangement commended itself to his judgement as simple and effecti e. His face had not been covered nor his eyes bandaged. He looked a moment at his 'unsteadfast footing,' then let his *gaze* wander to the swirling water of the stream racing madly beneath his feet. A piece of dancing driftwood caught his attention and his eyes followed it down the current. How slowly it appeared to move! What a sluggish stream!

He closed his eyes in order to fix his last thoughts upon his wife and children. The water, touched to gold by the early

Dignitary – *Notable*
Etiquette – *Manners*
Assassin – *Killer*
Condemned – *Blamed*

sun, the brooding mists under the banks at some distance down the stream, the fort, the soldiers, the piece of drift - all had distracted him. And now he became *conscious* of a new disturbance. Striking through the thought of his dear ones was sound which he could neither ignore nor understand, a sharp, *distinct*, metallic *percussion* like the stroke of a blacksmith's hammer upon the anvil; it had the same ringing quality. He wondered what it was, and whether immeasurably distant or near by - it seemed both. Its *recurrence* was regular, but as slow as the tolling of a death knell.

He awaited each new stroke with impatience and - he knew not why - *apprehension*. The intervals of silence grew progressively longer; the delays became maddening. With their greater infrequency the sounds increased in strength and sharpness. They hurt his ear like the trust of a knife; he feared he would shriek. What he heard was the ticking of his watch.

He unclosed his eyes and saw again the water below him. "If I could free my hands," he thought, "I might throw off the noose and spring into the stream. By diving I could *evade* the bullets and, swimming *vigorously*, reach the bank, take to the woods and get away home. My home, thank God, is as yet outside their lines; my wife and little ones are still beyond the invader's farthest advance."

As these thoughts, which have here to be set down in words, were flashed into the doomed man's brain rather than evolved from it the captain nodded to the sergeant. The sergeant stepped aside.

II

Peyton Fahrquhar was a well-to-do planter, of an old and highly respected Alabama family. Being a slave owner and like other slave owners a politician, he was naturally an original *secessionist* and *ardently* devoted to the Southern cause. Circumstances of an *imperious* nature, which it is unnecessary to relate here, had prevented him from taking service with that gallant army which had fought the *disastrous* campaigns ending with the fall of Corinth, and he chafed under the inglorious restraint, longing for the release of his energies, the larger life of the soldier, the opportunity for distinction. That opportunity, he felt, would come, as it comes to all in wartime.

Conscious – *Aware*
Percussion – *Drumming*
Recurrence – *Repetition*
Imperious – *Arrogant*

Meanwhile he did what he could. No service was too *humble* for him to perform in the aid of the South, no adventure to perilous for him to undertake if consistent with the character of a civilian who was at heart a soldier, and who in good faith and without too much qualification assented to at least a part of the frankly *villainous dictum* that all is fair in love and war.

One evening while Fahrquhar and his wife were sitting on a rustic bench near the entrance to his grounds, a gray-clad soldier rode up to the gate and asked for a drink of water. Mrs. Fahrquhar was only too happy to serve him with her own white hands. While she was fetching the water her husband approached the dusty horseman and *inquired* eagerly for news from the front.

"The Yanks are repairing the railroads," said the man, "and are getting ready for another advance. They have reached the Owl Creek bridge, put it in order and built a stockade on the north bank. The commandant has issued an order, which is posted everywhere, declaring that any civilian caught interfering with the railroad, its bridges, tunnels, or trains will be summarily hanged. I saw the order."

"How far is it to the Owl Creek bridge?" Fahrquhar asked.

"About thirty miles."

"Is there no force on this side of the creek?"

"Only a picket post half a mile out, on the railroad, and a single sentinel at this end of the bridge."

"Suppose a man - a civilian and student of hanging - should *elude* the picket post and perhaps get the bette of the sentinel," said Fahrquhar, smiling, "what could he accomplish?"

The soldier reflected. "I was there a month ago," he replied. "I observed that the flood of last winter had lodged great quantity of driftwood against the wooden pier at this end of the bridge. It is now dry and would burn like tinder."

The lady had now brought the water, which the soldier drank. He thanked her ceremoniously, bowed to her husband and rode away. An hour later, after nightfall, he re-passed the plantation, going northward in the direction from which he had come. He was a Federal scout.

Assented – *Acceptance*
Dictum – *Saying*
Picket – *Protest*
Ceremoniously – *Grandly*

III

As Peyton Fahrquhar fell straight downward through the bridge he lost consciousness and was as one already dead. From this state he was *awakened* - ages later, it seemed to him - by the pain of a sharp pressure upon his throat, followed by a sense of suffocation. Keen, *poignant agonies* seemed to shoot from his neck downward through every fiber of his body and limbs. These pains appeared to flash along well defined lines of *ramificatio* and to beat with an inconceivably *rapid* periodicity. They seemed like streams of pulsating fir heating him to an intolerable temperature.

As to his head, he was conscious of nothing but a feeling of fullness - of congestion. These sensations were unaccompanied by thought. The intellectual part of his nature was already *efface* ; he had power only to feel, and feeling was torment. He was conscious of motion. Encompassed in a luminous cloud, of which he was now merely the fiery heart, without material substance, he swung through unthinkable arcs of oscillation, like a vast pendulum. Then all at once, with terrible suddenness, the light about him shot upward with the noise of a loud splash; a frightful roaring was in his ears, and all was cold and dark.

The power of thought was restored; he knew that the rope had broken and he had fallen into the stream. There was no additional strangulation; the noose about his neck was already suffocating him and kept the water from his lungs. To die of hanging at the bottom of a river! - The idea seemed to him *ludicrous*. He opened his eyes in the darkness and saw above him a gleam of light, but how distant, how inaccessible! He was still sinking, for the light became fainter and fainter until it was a mere glimmer. Then it began to grow and brighten, and he knew that he was rising toward the surface - knew it with reluctance, for he was now very comfortable. "To be hanged and drowned," he thought, "that is not so bad; but I do not wish to be shot. No; I will not be shot; that is not fair."

He was not conscious of an effort, but a sharp pain in his wrist apprised him that he was trying to free his hands. He gave the struggle his attention, as an idler might observe the feat of a juggler, without interest in the outcome.

Poignant – *Emotional*
Agonies – *Miseries*
Ramifi ation – *Result*
Apprised – *Advised*

What splendid effort! What **magnificen**, what superhuman strength! Ah, that was a fine **endeavor**! Bravo! The cord fell away; his arms parted and floated upward, the hands dimly seen on each side in the growing light. He watched them with a new interest as first one and then the other pounced upon the noose at his neck. They tore it away and **thrust** it fiercely aside, its undulations resembling those of a water snake. "Put it back, put it back!" He thought he shouted these words to his hands, for the undoing of the noose had been succeeded by the direst pang that he had yet experienced. His neck ached horribly; his brain was on fire, his heart, which had been flu - tering faintly, gave a great leap, trying to force itself out at his mouth. His whole body was racked and wrenched with an insupportable **anguish**! But his disobedient hands gave no heed to the command.

They beat the water vigorously with quick, downward strokes, forcing him to the surface. He felt his head emerge; his eyes were blinded by the sunlight; his chest expanded convulsively, and with a supreme and crowning *agony* his lungs *engulfed* a great draught of air, which instantly he expelled in a shriek!

He was now in full possession of his physical senses. They were, indeed, preternaturally keen and alert. Something in the awful disturbance of his organic system had so exalted and refined them that they made record of things never before perceived. He felt the ripples upon his face and heard their separate sounds as they struck.

He looked at the forest on the bank of the stream, saw the individual trees, the leaves and the veining of each leaf - he saw the very insects upon them: the locusts, the brilliant bodied flies, the gray spiders stretching their webs from twig to twig. He noted the *prismatic* colors in all the dew drops upon a million blades of grass.

The humming of the gnats that danced above the eddies of the stream, the beating of the dragonflies' wings, the strokes of the water spiders' legs, like oars which had lifted their boat - all these made *audible* music. A fish slid along beneath his eyes and he heard the rush of its body parting the water.

He had come to the surface facing down the stream; in a moment the visible world seemed to wheel slowly round, himself the *pivotal* point, and he saw the bridge, the fort, the

Direst – *Critical*
Exalted – *Glorious*
Prismatic – *Bright*
Pivotal – *Essential*

soldiers upon the bridge, the captain, the sergeant, the two privates, his executioners.

They were in silhouette against the blue sky. They shouted and gesticulated, pointing at him. The captain had drawn his pistol, but did not fire; the others were unarmed. Their movements were *grotesque* and horrible, their forms gigantic.

Suddenly he heard a sharp report and something struck the water smartly within a few inches of his head, spatterin his face with spray. He heard a second report, and saw one of the sentinels with his rifle at his shoulder, a light cloud of blue smoke rising from the muzzle. The man in the water saw the eye of the man on the bridge gazing into his own through the sights of the rifle. He observed that it was a gray eye and remembered having read that gray eyes were keenest, and that all famous marksmen had them. Nevertheless, this one had missed.

A counter-swirl had caught Fahrquhar and turned him half round; he was again looking at the forest on the bank opposite the fort. The sound of a clear, high voice in a *monotonous singsong* now rang out behind him and came across the water with a distinctness that pierced and subdued all other sounds, even the beating of the ripples in his ears. Although no soldier, he had frequented camps enough to know the dread significance of that *deliberate*, drawling, *aspirated chant;* the lieutenant on shore was taking a part in the morning's work.

How coldly and pitilessly - with what an even, calm intonation, presaging, and enforcing *tranquillity* in the men - with what accurately measured interval fell those cruel words,

"Company! . . . Attention! . . . Shoulder arms! . . . Ready! . . . Aim! . . . Fire!"

Fahrquhar dived - dived as deeply as he could. The water roared in his ears like the voice of Niagara, yet he heard the dull thunder of the volley and, rising again toward the surface, met shining bits of metal, singularly flattened *oscillating* slowly downward. Some of them touched him on the face and hands, then fell away, continuing their descent. One lodged between his collar and neck; it was uncomfortably warm and he snatched it out.

As he rose to the surface, gasping for breath, he saw that he had been a long time under water; he was *perceptibly* farther downstream - nearer to safety. The soldiers had almost

Monotonous – *Dull*
Drawling – *Prolong*
Intonation – *Tone*
Presaging – *Prediction*

finished reloading; the metal ramrods flashed all at once in the sunshine as they were drawn from the barrels, turned in the air, and thrust into their sockets. The two sentinels fired again, independently and ineffectually

The hunted man saw all this over his shoulder; he was now swimming vigorously with the current. His brain was as energetic as his arms and legs; he thought with the rapidity of lightning,

"The officer, he reasoned, "will not make that martinet's error a second time. It is as easy to *dodge* a volley as a single shot. He has probably already given the command to fire at will. God help me, I cannot dodge them all!"

An appalling splash within two yards of him was followed by a loud, rushing sound, *diminuendo*, which seemed to travel back through the air to the fort and died in an explosion which stirred the very river to its deeps! A rising sheet of water curved over him, fell down upon him, blinded him, strangled him! The cannon had taken a hand in the game.

As he shook his head free from the commotion of the **smitte** water he heard the *deflecte* shot humming through the air ahead, and in an instant it was cracking and smashing the branches in the forest beyond.

"They will not do that again," he thought; "the next time they will use a charge of grape. I must keep my eye upon the gun; the smoke will *apprise* me - the report arrives too late; it lags behind the missile. That is a good gun."

Suddenly he felt himself whirled round and round - spinning like a top. The water, the banks, the forests, the now distant bridge, fort and men, all were *commingled* and blurred. Objects were represented by their colors only; circular horizontal streaks of color - that was all he saw. He had been caught in a **vortex** and was being whirled on with a velocity of advance and gyration that made him giddy and sick.

In few moments he was flung upon the gravel at the foot of the left bank of the stream - the southern bank - and behind a projecting point which *concealed* him from his enemies. The sudden arrest of his motion, the *abrasion* of one of his hands on the gravel, restored him, and he wept with delight. He dug his fingers into the sand, threw it over himself in handfuls and audibly blessed it.

Appalling – *Awful*
Diminuendo – *A gradual reduction of force, loudness*
Commingled – *Blend, combined*
Gyration – *Twist, rotation*

It looked like diamonds, rubies, emeralds; he could think of nothing beautiful which it did not resemble. The trees upon the bank were giant garden plants; he noted a definite order in their arrangement, inhaled the fragrance of their blooms. A strange *roseate* light shone through the spaces among their trunks and the wind made in their branches the music of Aeolian harps. He had not wish to perfect his escape - he was content to remain in that enchanting spot until retaken.

A whiz and a rattle of grapeshot among the branches high above his head roused him from his dream. The **baffl** cannoneer had fired him a random farewell. He sprang to his feet, rushed up the sloping bank, and plunged into the forest.

All that day he travelled, laying his course by the rounding sun. The forest seemed *interminable*; nowhere did he discover a break in it, not even a woodman's road. He had not known that he lived in so wild a region. There was something uncanny in the revelation.

By nightfall he was *fatigued*, footsore, and famished. The thought of his wife and children urged him on. At last he found a road which led him in what he knew to be the right direction. It was as wide and straight as a city street, yet it seemed untravelled. No fields bordered it, no dwelling anywhere. Not so much as the barking of a dog suggested human habitation. The black bodies of the trees formed a straight wall on both sides, terminating on the horizon in a point, like a diagram in a lesson in *perspective*.

Overhead, as he looked up through this rift in the wood, shone great golden stars looking unfamiliar and grouped in strange constellations. He was sure they were arranged in some order which had a secret and *malign* significance. The wood on either side was full of singular noises, among which - once, twice, and again - he distinctly heard whispers in an unknown tongue.

His neck was in pain and lifting his hand to it found it horribly swollen. He knew that it had a circle of black where the rope had bruised it. His eyes felt congested; he could no longer close them. His tongue was swollen with thirst; he relieved its fever by thrusting it forward from between his teeth into the cold air. How softly the turf had carpeted the untravelled avenue - he could no longer feel the roadway beneath his feet!

Revelation – *Exposure*
Famished – *Starving, extremely hungry*
Malign – *Criticize*
Delirium – *Mental confusion*

Doubtless, despite his suffering, he had fallen asleep while walking, for now he sees another scene - perhaps he has merely recovered from a delirium. He stands at the gate of his own home. All is as he left it, and all bright and beautiful in the morning sunshine. He must have travelled the entire night. As he pushes open the gate and passes up the wide white walk, he sees a flutte of female garments; his wife, looking fresh and cool and sweet, steps down from the veranda to meet him. At the bottom of the steps she stands waiting, with a smile of ineffable joy, an attitude of matchless grace and dignity. Ah, how beautiful she is! He springs forwards with extended arms. As he is about to clasp her he feels a stunning blow upon the back of the neck; a blinding white light blazes all about him with a sound like the shock of a cannon - then all is darkness and silence!

Peyton Fahrquhar was dead; his body, with a broken neck, swung gently from side to side beneath the timbers of the Owl Creek bridge.

Food For Thought

When Peyton Farquhar was being hanged, the rope broke, and then he fell into the water and waded his way through a forest to his home to meet his loved ones - his wife and children. Later, we come to know that it's all his imagination and he never escaped death. Do you think that a man's last wish is always fulfilled by God? If this is true, what would be your last wish and why?

Dignity – *Bearing, self-respect*
Ineffable – *In expressible*
Stunning – *Astounding, stupefying*
Flutter – **Vibrate**

The Realm Of The Unreal
Ambrose Bierce

I

FOr a part of the distance between Auburn and Newcastle the road -- first on one side of a creek and then on the other -- occupies the whole bottom of the ravine, being partly cut out of the steep hillside, and partly built up with boulders removed from the creek-bed by the miners. The hills are wooded, the course of the ravine is **sinuous**. In a dark night careful driving is required in order not to go off into the water.

The night that I have in memory was dark, the creek a torrent, swollen by a recent storm. I had driven up from Newcastle and was within about a mile of Auburn in the darkest and narrowest part of the ravine, looking intently ahead of my horse for the roadway. Suddenly I saw a man almost under the animal's nose, and reined in with a jerk that came near setting the creature upon its haunches.

'I beg your pardon,' I said; 'I did not see you, sir.'

'You could hardly be expected to see me,' the man replied civilly, approaching the side of the vehicle; 'and the noise of the creek prevented my hearing you.'

I at once recognized the voice, although fi e years had passed since I had heard it. I was not particularly well pleased to hear it now.

'You are Dr. Dorrimore, I think,' said I.

'Yes; and you are my good friend Mr. Manrich. I am more than glad to see you -- the excess,' he added, with a light laugh, 'being due to the fact that I am going your way, and naturally expect an invitation to ride with you.'

'Which I extend with all my heart.'

That was not altogether true.

Dr. Dorrimore thanked me as he seated himself beside me, and I drove cautiously forward, as before. Doubtless it is fancy, but it seems to me now that the remaining distance

Boulders – *Stones*
Sinuous – *Twisting*
Forbidding – *Threatening, grim*
Desolate – *Deserted, lonely*

was made in a chill fog; that I was uncomfortably cold; that the way was longer than ever before, and the town, when we reached it, cheerless, forbidding, and **desolate**. It must have been early in the evening, yet I do not recollect a light in any of the houses nor a living thing in the streets. Dorrimore explained at some length how he happened to be there, and where he had been during the years that had elapsed since I had seen him.

I recall the fact of the narrative, but none of the facts narrated. He had been in foreign countries and had returned -- this is all that my memory retains, and this I already knew. As to myself I cannot remember that I spoke a word, though doubtless I did.

Of one thing I am distinctly conscious -- the man's presence at my side was strangely distasteful and disquieting -- so much so that when I at last pulled up under the lights of the Putnam House I experienced a sense of having escaped some spiritual *peril* of a nature peculiarly forbidding. This sense of relief was somewhat modified by the discovery that Dr. Dorrimore was living at the same hotel.

II

In partial explanation of my feelings regarding Dr. Dorrimore I will relate briefly the circumstances under which I had met him some years before. One evening a half-dozen men of whom I was one were sitting in the library of the Bohemian Club in San Francisco. The conversation had turned to the subject of sleight-of-hand and the feats of the prestidigitateurs, one of whom was then exhibiting at a local theatre.

'These fellows are pretenders in a double sense,' said one of the party; 'they can do nothing which it is worth one's while to be made a *dupe* by. The *humblest* wayside juggler in India could mystify them to the verge of *lunacy*.'

'For example, how?' asked another, lighting a cigar.

'For example, by all their common and familiar performances -- throwing large objects into the air which never come down; causing plants to sprout, grow visibly and blossom, in

Elapsed – *Gone*
Retains – *Cling to*
Modifi d – *Tailored, amended*

bare ground chosen by spectators; putting a man into a wicker basket, piercing him through and through with a sword while he shrieks and bleeds, and then -- the basket being opened nothing is there; tossing the free end of a silken ladder into the air, mounting it and disappearing.'

'Nonsense!' I said, rather *uncivilly*, I fear. 'You surely do not believe such things?'

'Certainly not. I have seen them too often.'

'But I do,' said a journalist of considerable local fame as a picturesque reporter. 'I have so frequently related them that nothing but observation could shake my *conviction*. Why, gentlemen, I have my own word for it.'

Nobody laughed -- all were looking at something behind me. Turning in my seat I saw a man in evening dress who had just entered the room. He was exceedingly dark, almost *swarthy*, with a thin face, black-bearded to the lips, an abundance of coarse black hair in some disorder, a high nose and eyes that glittered with as soulless an expression as those of a cobra.

One of the group rose and introduced him as Dr. Dorrimore, of Calcutta. As each of us was presented in turn he acknowledged the fact with a profound bow in the Oriental manner, but with nothing of Oriental gravity. His smile impressed me as cynical and a trifle *contemptuous*. His whole demeanour I can describe only as disagreeably engaging.

His presence led the conversation into other channels. He said little -- I do not recall anything of what he did say. I thought his voice singularly rich and melodious, but it affecte me in the same way as his eyes and smile. In a few minutes I rose to go. He also rose and put on his overcoat.

'Mr. Manrich,' he said, 'I am going your way.'

'The devil you are!' I thought. 'How do you know which way I am going?' Then I said, 'I shall be pleased to have your company.'

We left the building together. No cabs were in sight, the street cars had gone to bed, there was a full moon and the cool night air was delightful; we walked up the California Street

Swarthy – *Dark complexioned*
Cynical – *Pessimistic, sascastic*
Trifle – *Of very little value, trivial*
Demeanor – *Manner, behaviour, conduct.*

Hill. I took that direction thinking he would naturally wish to take another, toward one of the hotels.

'You do not believe what is told of the Hindu jugglers,' he said *abruptly*.

'How do you know that?' I asked.

Without replying he laid his hand lightly upon my arm and with the other pointed to the stone sidewalk directly in front. There, almost at our feet, lay the dead body of a man, the face upturned and white in the moonlight! A sword whose hilt sparkled with gems stood fixed and upright in the breast; a pool of blood had collected on the stones of the sidewalk.

I was startled and terrified -- not only by what I saw, but by the circumstances under which I saw it. Repeatedly during our ascent of the hill my eyes, I thought, had traversed the whole reach of that sidewalk, from street to street. How could they have been insensible to this *dreadful* object now so conspicuous in the white moonlight.

As my dazed faculties cleared I observed that the body was in evening dress; the overcoat thrown wide open revealed the dress-coat, the white tie, the broad expanse of shirt front pierced by the sword. And -- horrible revelation! The face, except for its pallor, was that of my companion! It was to the minutest detail of dress and feature Dr. Dorrimore himself. *Bewildered* and horrified, I turned to look for the living man. He was nowhere visible, and with an added terror I retired from the place, down the hill in the direction whence I had come. I had taken but a few strides when a strong grasp upon my shoulder arrested me.

I came near crying out with terror: the dead man, the sword still fixed in his breast, stood beside me! Pulling out the sword with his disengaged hand, he flung it from him, the moonlight glinting upon the jewels of its hilt and the unsullied steel of its blade. It fell with a clang upon the sidewalk ahead and -- vanished! The man, swarthy as before, relaxed his grasp upon my shoulder and looked at me with the same *cynical* regard that I had observed on first meeting him. The dead have not that look -- it partly restored me, and turning

Conspicuous – *Obvious*
Strides – *To walk long steps*
Disengaged – *Detached, to free oneself*

my head backward, I saw the smooth white expanse of sidewalk, unbroken from street to street.

'What is all this nonsense, you devil?' I demanded, fiercely enough, though weak and trembling in every limb.

'It is what some are pleased to call jugglery,' he answered, with a light, hard laugh.

He turned down Dupont Street and I saw him no more until we met in the Auburn ravine.

III

On the day after my second meeting with Dr. Dorrimore I did not see him. The clerk in the Putnam House explained that a slight illness confined him to his rooms. That afternoon at the railway station I was surprised and made happy by the unexpected arrival of Miss Margaret Corray and her mother, from Oakland.

This is not a love story. I am no story teller, and love as it is cannot be portrayed in a literature dominated and **enthralled** by the debasing *tyranny* which 'sentences letters' in the name of the Young Girl. Under the Young Girl's blighting reign -- or rather under the rule of those false Ministers of the Censure who have appointed themselves to the custody of her welfare -- Love

veils her sacred fires

And, unaware, Morality expires,

famished upon the sifted meal and distilled water of a *prudish* purveyance.

Let it suffic that Miss Corray and I were engaged in marriage. She and her mother went to the hotel at which I lived, and for two weeks I saw her daily. That I was happy needs hardly be said; the only bar to my perfect enjoyment of those golden days was the presence of Dr. Dorrimore, whom I had felt compelled to introduce to the ladies.

By them he was evidently held in favour. What could I say? I knew absolutely nothing to his *discredit*. His manners were those of a cultivated and considerate gentleman; and to women a man's manner is the man. On one or two occasions

---

Enthralled – *Enchanted*
Debasing – *Humiliating*
Blighting – *Destroying, spoiling, disappointing*
Purveyance – *Supply*
Discredit – *Dishonor*
Calumny – *Lie, slander, defamation*

when I saw Miss Corray walking with him I was furious, and once had the indiscretion to protest.

Asked for reasons, I had none to give, and fancied I saw in her expression a shade of contempt for the vagaries of a jealous mind. In time I grew morose and consciously disagreeable, and resolved in my madness to return to San Francisco the next day. Of this, however, I said nothing.

IV

There was at Auburn an old, abandoned cemetery. It was nearly in the heart of the town, yet by night it was as gruesome a place as the most dismal of human moods could crave. The railings about the plots were prostrate, *decayed*, or altogether gone. Many of the graves were sunken, from others grew sturdy pines, whose roots had committed unspeakable sin. The headstones were fallen and broken across; brambles overran the ground; the fence was mostly gone, and cows and pigs wandered there at will; the place was a dishonour to the living, a *calumny* on the dead, a *blasphemy* against God.

The evening of the day on which I had taken my madman's resolution to depart in anger from all that was dear to me found me in that congenial spot. The light of the half moon fell ghostly through the foliage of trees in spots and patches, revealing much that was unsightly, and the black shadows seemed conspiracies withholding to the proper time revelations of darker import.

Passing along what had been a gravel path, I saw emerging from shadow the figure of Dr. Dorrimore. I was myself in shadow, and stood still with clenched hands and set teeth, trying to control the impulse to leap upon and strangle him. A moment later a second figure joined him and clung to his arm. It was Margaret Corray!

I cannot rightly relate what occurred. I know that I sprang forward, bent upon murder; I know that I was found in the grey of the morning, bruised and bloody, with finge marks upon my throat. I was taken to the Putnam House, where for days I lay in a *delirium*. All this I know, for I have

Congenial – *Friendly*
Conspiracies – *Secret plans to do something illegal, plot*
Convalescence – *Restoration*
Petulantly – *Sullenly*

been told. And of my own knowledge I know that when consciousness returned with *convalescence* I sent for the clerk of the hotel.

'Are Mrs. Corray and her daughter still here?' I asked.

'What name did you say?'

'Corray.'

'Nobody by that name has been here.'

'I beg you will not *trifl* with me,' I said *petulantly*. 'You see that I am all right now; tell me the truth.'

'I give you my word,' he replied with evident sincerity, 'we have had no guests of that name.'

His words *stupefie* me. I lay for a few moments in silence; then I asked. 'Where is Dr. Dorrimore?'

'He left on the morning of your fight and has not been heard of since. It was a rough deal he gave you.'

V

Such are the facts of this case. Margaret Corray is now my wife. She has never seen Auburn, and during the weeks whose history as it shaped itself in my brain I have endeavoured to relate, was living at her home in Oakland, wondering where her lover was and why he did not write. The other day I saw in the Baltimore Sun the following paragraph:

'Professor Valentine Dorrimore, the hypnotist, had a large audience last night. The lecturer, who has lived most of his life in India, gave some marvellous exhibitions of his power, hypnotizing anyone who chose to submit himself to the experiment, by merely looking at him. In fact, he twice hypnotized the entire audience (reporters alone exempted), making all entertain the most extraordinary illusions.

The most valuable feature of the lecture was the disclosure of the methods of the Hindu jugglers in their famous performances, familiar in the mouths of travellers. The professor declares that these thaumaturgists have *acquired* such skill in the art which he learned at their feet that they perform their miracles by simply throwing the "spectators" into a state of

Exempted – *Relieved*
Illusions – *False appearances*
Thaumaturgists – *Sorcerers*
Susceptible – *Vulnerable*

hypnosis and telling them what to see and hear. His *assertion* that a peculiarly susceptible subject may be kept in the realm of the unreal for weeks, months, and even years, dominated by whatever delusions and hallucinations the operator may from time to time suggest, is a **trifl** disquieting.'

Food For Thought

In this story, the author has emphasised and proved that jugglery and hypnotism do exist if one has the power to hypnotise anyone who chooses to submit oneself to such experiments. Have you ever experienced such situations in your life or heard any other such real - life story? Narrate it in brief.

A Psychological Shipwreck
— Ambrose Bierce

IN the summer of 1874 I was in Liverpool, whither I had gone on business for the mercantile house of Bronson & Jarrett, New York. I am William Jarrett; my partner was Zenas Bronson. The firm failed last year, and unable to **endure** the fall from affluence to p erty he died.

Having finished my business, and feeling the lassitude and exhaustion incident to its dispatch, I felt that a protracted sea voyage would be both agreeable and beneficial, so instead of **embarking** for my return on one of the many fine passenger steamers I booked for New York on the sailing vessel Morrow, upon which I had shipped a large and valuable invoice of the goods I had bought.

The Morrow was an English ship with, of course, but little accommodation for passengers, of whom there were only myself, a young woman and her servant, who was a middle-aged negress.

I thought it singular that a travelling English girl should be so attended, but she afterward explained to me that the woman had been left with her family by a man and his wife from South Carolina, both of whom had died on the same day at the house of the young lady's father in Devonshire -- a circumstance in itself sufficientl uncommon to remain rather distinctly in my memory, even had it not afterward transpired in conversation with the young lady that the name of the man was William Jàrrett, the same as my own. I knew that a branch of my family had settled in South Carolina, but of them and their history I was ignorant.

The Morrow sailed from the mouth of the Mersey on the 15th of June, and for several weeks we had fair breezes and unclouded skies. The skipper, an admirable seaman but nothing more, favoured us with very little of his society, except at his table; and the young woman, Miss Janette Harford, and I became very well **acquainted**.

We were, in truth, nearly always together, and being of an **introspective** turn of mind I often endeavoured to analyse and define the novel feeling with which she inspired me -- a

Mercantile – *Commercial*
Lassitude – *Tiredness*
Protracted – *Extended*
Transpired – *Emerged, evolved*

secret, subtle, but powerful attraction which constantly impelled me to seek her; but the attempt was hopeless. I could only be sure that at least it was not love. Having assured myself of this and being certain that she was quite as wholehearted, I ventured one evening (I remember it was on the 3rd of July) as we sat on deck to ask her, laughingly, if she could assist me to resolve my psychological doubt.

For a moment she was silent, with averted face, and I began to fear I had been extremely rude and indelicate; then she fixed her eyes gravely on my own. In an instant my mind was dominated by as strange a fancy as ever entered human consciousness. It seemed as if she were looking at me, not with, but through, those eyes -- from an immeasurable distance behind them -- and that a number of other persons, men, women and children, upon whose faces I caught strangely familiar evanescent expressions, clustered about her, struggling with gentle eagerness to look at me through the same orbs. Ship, ocean, sky -- all had vanished. I was conscious of nothing but the figures in this extraordinary and fantastic scene.

Then all at once darkness fell upon me, and anon from out of it, as to one who grows accustomed by degrees to a dimmer light, my former surroundings of deck and mast and cordage slowly resolved themselves. Miss Harford had closed her eyes and was leaning back in her chair, apparently asleep, the book she had been reading open in her lap.

Impelled by surely I cannot say what motive, I glanced at the top of the page; it was a copy of that rare and curious work, Denneker's Meditations, and the lady's index finge rested on this passage:

'To sundry it is given to be drawn away, and to be apart from the body for a season; for, as concerning rills which would flow across each other the weaker is borne along by the stronger, so there be certain of kin whose paths intersecting, their souls do bear company, the while their bodies go fore-appointed ways, unknowing.'

Miss Harford arose, shuddering; the sun had sunk below the horizon, but it was not cold. There was not a breath of wind; there were no clouds in the sky, yet not a star was visible. A hurried tramping sounded on the deck; the captain, summoned

Gravely – *Sternly*
Evanescent – *Passing*
Sundry – *Various*
Exclaim – *Cry out*

from below, joined the first officer who stood looking at the barometer. 'Good God!' I heard him exclaim.

An hour later the form of Janette Harford, invisible in the darkness and spray, was torn from my grasp by the cruel vortex of the sinking ship, and I fainted in the cordage of the floaing mast to which I had lashed myself.

It was by lamplight that I awoke. I lay in a berth amid the familiar surroundings of the state-room of a steamer. On a couch opposite sat a man, half undressed for bed, reading a book.

I recognized the face of my friend Gordon Doyle, whom I had met in Liverpool on the day of my embarkation, when he was himself about to sail on the steamer City of Prague, on which he had urged me to accompany him.

After some moments I now spoke his name. He simply said, 'Well,' and turned a leaf in his book without removing his eyes from the page.

'Doyle,' I repeated, 'did they save her? '

He now deigned to look at me and smiled as if amused. He evidently thought me but half awake.

'Her? Whom do you mean?'

'Janette Harford.'

His amusement turned to amazement; he stared at me fixedly, saying nothing

'You will tell me after awhile,' I continued; 'I suppose you will tell me after awhile.'

A moment later I asked, 'What ship is this?' Doyle stared again. 'The steamer City of Prague, bound from Liverpool to New York, three weeks out with a broken shaft. Principal passenger, Mr. Gordon Doyle; ditto lunatic, Mr. William Jarrett. These two distinguished travellers embarked together, but they are about to part, it being the resolute intention of the former to pitch the latter o erboard.'

I sat bolt upright. 'Do you mean to say that I have been for three weeks a passenger on this steamer?'

'Yes, pretty nearly; this is the 3rd of July.'

'Have I been ill?'

'Right as a trivet all the time, and punctual at your meals.'

Deigned – *Lower yourself*
Resolute – *Firm*
Intention – *Purpose*
Trivet – *A special knife for cutting pile loops*

'My God! Doyle, there is some mystery here; do have the goodness to be serious. Was I not rescued from the wreck of the ship Morrow?'

Doyle changed colour, and approaching me, laid his fi - gers on my wrist. A moment later, 'What do you know of Janette Harford?' he asked ery calmly.

'First tell me what you know of her?'

Mr. Doyle gazed at me for some moments as if thinking what to do, then seating himself again on the couch, said,

'Why should I not? I am engaged to marry Janette Harford, whom I met a year ago in London. Her family, one of the wealthiest in Devonshire, cut up rough about it, and we eloped -- are eloping rather, for on the day that you and I walked to the landing stage to go aboard this steamer she and her faithful servant, a negress, passed us, driving to the ship Morrow.

She would not **consent** to go in the same vessel with me, and it had been deemed best that she take a sailing vessel in order to avoid observation and lessen the risk of detection. I am now alarmed lest this cursed breaking of our machinery may detain us so long that the Morrow will get to New York before us, and the poor girl will not know where to go.'

I lay still in my berth -- so still I hardly breathed. But the subject was evidently not **displeasing** to Doyle, and after a short pause he resumed,

'By the way, she is only an adopted daughter of the Harfords. Her mother was killed at their place by being thrown from a horse while hunting, and her father, mad with grief, made away with himself the same day. No one ever claimed the child, and after a reasonable time they adopted her. She has grown up in the belief that she is their daughter.'

'Doyle, what book are you reading?'

'Oh, it's called Denneker's Meditations. It's a rum lot, Janette gave it to me; she happened to have two copies. Want to see it?'

Eloping – *Escaping*
Deemed – *Supposed*
Lest – *In case*
Rills – *Streams or small rivulets, brooks*

He tossed me the volume, which opened as it fell. On one of the exposed pages was a marked passage,

'To sundry it is given to be drawn away, and to be apart from the body for a season; for, as concerning rills which would flow across each other the weaker is borne along by the stronger, so there be certain of kin whose paths intersecting, their souls do bear company, the while their bodies go foreappointed ways, unknowing.'

'She had -- she has -- a singular taste in reading,' I managed to say, mastering my **agitation**.

'Yes. And now perhaps you will have the kindness to explain how you knew her name and that of the ship she sailed in.'

'You talked of her in your sleep,' I said.

A week later we were towed into the port of New York. But the Morrow was never heard from.

Food For Thought

The narrator and Doyle, both had walked to the landing stage to go aboard the same steamer called the City of Prague. Then how did the narrator come across Miss Janette Harford on the ship called 'Morrow' which sailed several weeks before the city of Prague? Do you think that the narrator was never in the 'Morrow' and had encountered with the ghost of Miss Janette Harford?

The Baby Tramp
— Ambrose Bierce

Blackburg

IF you had seen little Jo standing at the street corner in the rain, you would hardly have admired him. It was apparently an ordinary autumn rainstorm, but the water which fell upon Jo (who was hardly old enough to be either just or unjust, and so perhaps did not come under the law of impartial distribution) appeared to have some property peculiar to itself: one would have said it was dark and adhesive -- sticky. But that could hardly be so, even in Blackburg, where things certainly did occur that were a good deal out of the common.

For example, ten or twelve years before, a shower of small frogs had fallen, as is credibly attested by a *contemporaneous* chronicle, the record concluding with a somewhat *obscure* statement to the effect that the chronicler considered it good growing-weather for Frenchmen.

Some years later, Blackburg had a fall of crimson snow; it is cold in Blackburg when winter is on, and the snows are frequent and deep. There can be no doubt of it -- the snow in this instance was of the colour of blood and melted into water of the same hue, if water it was, not blood. The phenomenon had attracted wide attention, and science had as many explanations as there were scientists who knew nothing about it. But the men of Blackburg--men who for many years had lived right there where the red snow fell, and might be supposed to know a good deal about the matter--shook their heads and said something would come of it

And something did, for the next summer was made memorable by the *prevalence* of a mysterious disease--epidemic, endemic, or the Lord knows what, though the physicians didn't--which carried away a full half of the population. Most of the other half carried themselves away and were slow to return, but finally came back, and were now increasing and multiplying as before, but Blackburg had not since been altogether the same.

Of quite another kind, though equally 'out of the common,' was the incident of Hetty Parlow's ghost. Hetty Parlow's maiden name had been Brownon, and in Blackburg that meant more than one would think.

Peculiar – *Strange*
Contemporaneous – *Originating*
Obscure – *Not known about*
Prevalence – *Occurrence*

The Brownons had from time *immemorial*--from the very earliest of the old colonial days--been the leading family of the town. It was the richest and it was the best, and Blackburg would have shed the last drop of its plebeian blood in defence of the Brownon fair fame. As few of the family's members had ever been known to live permanently away from Blackburg, although most of them were educated elsewhere and nearly all had travelled, there was quite a number of them. The men held most of the public offices and the women were foremost in all good works. Of the latter, Hetty was most beloved by reason of the sweetness of her *disposition*, the purity of her character and her singular personal beauty. She married in Boston a young scape-grace named Parlow, and like a good Brownon brought him to Blackburg forthwith and made a man and a town councillor of him. They had a child which they named Joseph and dearly loved, as was then the fashion among parents in that region. Then they died of the mysterious disorder already mentioned, and at the age of one whole year Joseph set up as an orphan.

Unfortunately for Joseph, the disease which had cut off his parents did not stop at that; it went on and *extirpated* nearly the whole Brownon contingent and its allies by marriage; and those who fled did not return. The tradition was broken, the Brownon estates passed into alien hands, and the only Brownons remaining in that place were underground in Oak Hill Cemetery, where, indeed, was a colony of them powerful enough to resist the *encroachment* of surrounding tribes and hold the best part of the grounds. But about the ghost:

One night, about three years after the death of Hetty Parlow, a number of the young people of Blackburg were passing Oak Hill Cemetery in a wagon--if you have been there you will remember that the road to Greenton runs alongside it on the south. They had been attending a May Day festival at Greenton; and that serves to fix the date. Altogether there may have been a dozen, and a jolly party they were, considering the legacy of gloom left by the town's recent sombre experiences. As they passed the cemetery, the man driving suddenly reined in his team with an exclamation of surprise. It was sufficientl surprising, no doubt, for just ahead, and almost at the roadside, though inside the cemetery, stood the ghost of Hetty Parlow. There could be no doubt of it, for she had been personally known to every youth and maiden in the party. That established the thing's identity; its character as ghost was signified by all the customary signs--the shroud, the long, undone hair,

Immemorial –
Ancient
Disposition –
Personality
Extirpated – *To destroy totally*
Encroachment – *Infringement*

the 'far-away look'--everything. This disquieting *apparition* was stretching out its arms towards the west, as if in supplication for the evening star, which, certainly, was an alluring object, though obviously out of reach. As they all sat silent (so the story goes) every member of that party of merrymakers--they had merry made on coffee and lemonade only--distinctly heard that ghost call the name 'Joey, Joey!' A moment later nothing was there. Of course, one does not have to believe all that.

Now, at that moment, as was afterward ascertained, Joey was wandering about in the sagebrush on the opposite side of the continent, near Winnemucca, in the State of Nevada. He had been taken to that town by some good persons distantly related to his dead father, and by them adopted and tenderly cared for. But on that evening, the poor child had strayed from home and was lost in the desert.

His after history is involved in obscurity and has gaps which *conjecture* alone can fill. It is known that he was found by a family of Piute Indians, who kept the little wretch with them for a time and then sold him--actually sold him for money to a woman on one of the east-bound trains, at a station a long way from Winnemucca. The woman professed to have made all manner of inquiries, but all in vain; so, being childless and a widow, she adopted him herself. At this point of his career Jo seemed to be getting a long way from the condition of orphanage; the interposition of a *multitude* of parents between himself and that woeful state promised him a long immunity from its disadvantages.

Mrs. Darnell, his newest mother, lived in Cleveland, Ohio. But her adopted son did not long remain with her. He was seen one afternoon by a policeman, new to that beat, deliberately toddling away from her house, and being questioned answered that he was 'a doin' home.' He must have travelled by rail, somehow, for three days later he was in the town of Whiteville, which, as you know, is a long way from Blackburg. His clothing was in pretty fair condition, but he was sinfully dirty. Unable to give any account of himself, he was arrested as a vagrant and sentenced to imprisonment in the Infants' Sheltering Home--where he was washed. Jo ran away from the Infants' Sheltering Home at Whiteville--just took to the woods one day, and the Home knew him no more forever.

 We find him next, or rather get back to him, standing forlorn in the cold autumn rain at a suburban street corner in

Apparition - *Person/Thing*
Shroud - *Covering*
Disquieting - *Disturbing*
Conjecture - *Speculation*
Multitude - *Gathering*

Blackburg; and it seems right to explain now that the raindrops falling upon him there were really not dark and gummy; they only failed to make his face and hands less so. Jo was indeed fearfully and wonderfully **besmirched**, as by the hand of an artist. And the *forlorn* little tramp had no shoes; his feet were bare, red, and swollen, and when he walked he limped with both legs. As to clothing--ah, you would hardly have had the skill to name any single garment that he wore, or say by what magic he kept it upon him. That he was cold all over and all through did not admit of a doubt; he knew it himself. Anyone would have been cold there that evening; but, for that reason, no one else was there. How Jo came to be there himself, he could not for the flickering little life of him have told, even if gifted with a vocabulary exceeding a hundred words. From the way he stared about him one could have seen that he had not the faintest notion of where (nor why) he was.

Yet he was not altogether a fool in his day and generation; being cold and hungry, and still able to walk a little by bending his knees very much indeed and putting his feet down toes first, he decided to enter one of the houses which flanke the street at long intervals and looked so bright and warm. But when he attempted to act upon that very sensible decision a burly dog came browsing out and disputed his right. Inexpressibly frightened, and believing, no doubt (with some reason, too), that brutes without meant brutality within, he hobbled away from all the houses, and with grey, wet field to right of him and grey, wet fields to left of him--with the rain half blinding him and the night coming in mist and darkness, held his way along the road that leads to Greenton. That is to say, the road leads those to Greenton who succeed in passing the Oak Hill Cemetery. A considerable number every year do not.

Jo did not.

They found him there the next morning, very wet, very cold, but no longer hungry. He had apparently entered the cemetery gate--hoping, perhaps, that it led to a house where there was no dog--and gone blundering about in the darkness, falling over many a grave, no doubt, until he had tired of it all and given up. The little body lay upon one side, with one **soiled** cheek upon one soiled hand, the other hand **tucked** away among the rags to make it warm, the other cheek washed clean and white at last, as for a kiss from one of God's great

---

Besmirched - *To soil/Tarnish*
Forlorn – *Lonely and sad*
Flickering – *To move waveringly*
Brutality – *The state of being ruthless, cruel, harsh*
Browsing – *To inspect something leisurely and casually*

angels. It was observed--though nothing was thought of it at the time, the body being as yet *unidentifie* --that the littl fellow was lying upon the grave of Hetty Parlow. The grave, however, had not opened to receive him. That is a circumstance which, without actual *irreverence*, one may wish had been ordered otherwise. Food For Thought

Food For Thought

Why did Hetty Parlow's ghost wander in and around the Oak Hill Cemetery? Why did the merrymakers hear the name, 'Joey, Joey?' Do you believe that a mother, is always a mother, whether dead or alive? How do you relate this statement with this story?

Soiled – *Stained*
Unidentifi d – *Anonymous*
Tucked – *To gather up and fold,*
Irreverence – *A disrespectful act or remark*

The Secret of Macarger's Gulch
~ Ambrose Bierce

NOrthwestwardly from Indian Hill, about nine miles as the crow flies, is Macarger's Gulch. It is not much of a gulch -- a mere *depression* between two wooded ridges of inconsiderable height. From its mouth up to its head -- for gulches, like rivers, have an anatomy of their own -- the distance does not exceed two miles, and the width at botto is at only one place more than a dozen yards; for most of the distance on either side of the little brook which drains it in winter, and goes dry in the early spring, there is no level ground at all; the steep slopes of the hills, covered with an almost *inpenetrable* growth of *manzanita* and *chemisal*, are parted by nothing but the width of the watercourse. No one but an occasional *enterprising* hunter of the vicinity ever goes into Macarger's Gulch, and fi e miles away it is unknown, even by name. Within that distance in any direction are far more conspicuous *topographical* features without names, and one might try in vain to ascertain by local inquiry the origin of the name of this one.

About midway between the head and the mouth of Macarger's Gulch, the hill on the right as you ascend is cloven by another gulch, a short dry one, and at the junction of the two is a level space of two or three acres, and there a few years ago stood an old board house containing one small room. How the component parts of the house, few and simple as they were, had been assembled at that almost inaccessible point is a problem in the solution of which there would be greater satisfaction than advantage. Possibly the creek bed is a reformed road. It is certain that the gulch was at one time pretty **thoroughly** prospected by miners, who must have had some means of gettin in with at least pack animals carrying tools and supplies; their profits, apparently, were not such as would have justified any considerable outlay to connect Macarger's Gulch with any centre of civilization enjoying the distinction of a sawmill. The house, however, was there, most of it. It lacked a door and a window frame, and the chimney of mud and stones had fallen into an unlovely heap, overgrown with rank weeds. Such humble furniture as there may once have been and much of the lower

Depression - *Dejcetion*
Impenetrable - *Inaccessible*
manzanita - *North Amercian strubs small trees*
Chemical - *A substance produced in a chemical process*
Enterprising - *Ambitious*
Topographical - *Relief features*
Thoroughly - *Minutely*

weather-boarding, had served as fuel in the camp fires of hunters; as had also, probably, the **kerbing** of an old well, which at the time I write of existed in the form of a rather wide but not very deep depression near by.

One afternoon in the summer of 1874, I passed up Macarger's Gulch from the narrow valley into which it opens, by following the dry bed of the brook. I was quail-shooting and had made a bag of about a dozen birds by the time I had reached the house described, of whose existence I was until then unaware. After rather carelessly **inspecting** the ruin I resumed my sport, and having fairly good success prolonged it until near sunset, when it occurred to me that I was a long way from any human **habitation** -- too far to reach one by nightfall. But in my game bag was food, and the old house would **affor** shelter, if shelter were needed on a warm and dewless night in the foothills of the Sierra Nevada, where one may sleep in comfort on the pine needles, without covering. I am fond of solitude and love the night, so my resolution to 'camp out' was soon taken, and by the time that it was dark I had made my bed of **boughs** and grasses in a corner of the room and was roasting a quail at a fire that I had kindled on the hearth. The smoke escaped out of the ruined chimney, the light **illuminated** the room with a kindly glow, and as I ate my simple meal of plain bird and drank the remains of a bottle of red wine which had served me all the afternoon in place of the water, which the region did not supply, I experienced a sense of comfort which better fare and accommodations do not al ays give.

Nevertheless, there was something lacking. I had a sense of comfort, but not of security. I detected myself **staring** more frequently at the open doorway and blank window than I could fin warrant for doing. Outside these apertures all was black, and I was unable to repress a certain feeling of apprehension as my fancy pictured the outer world and filled it with unfriendly entities, natural and supernatural -- chief among which, in their respective classes were the **grizzly** bear, which I knew was occasionally still seen in that region, and the ghost, which I had reason to think was not. Unfortunately, our feelings do not always respect the law of probabilities, and to me that evening, the possible and the impossible were equally disquieting.

Every one who has had experience in the matter must have observed that one confronts the actual and imaginary perils of the night with far less **apprehension** in the open air than in a house

Kerbing - *Bending Curving*
Inspecting - *Examining*
Habitation - *A place of residence*
Aff rd - *To manage*
Boughs - *Branches*
Grizzly - *Greyish*

with an open doorway. I felt this now as I lay on my leafy couch in a corner of the room next to the chimney and permitted my fire to die out. So strong became my sense of the presence of something *malign* and menacing in the place, that I found myself almost unable to withdraw my eyes from the opening, as in the deepening darkness it became more and more *indistinct*. And when the last little flame flickered and went out I *grasped* the shotgun which I had laid at my side and actually turned the *muzzle* in the direction of the now invisible entrance, my thumb on one of the hammers, ready to cock the piece, my breath suspended, my muscles rigid and tense. But later I laid down the weapon with a sense of shame and mortification. What did I fear, and why? -- I, to whom the night had been a more familiar face than that of man –

I, in whom that element of hereditary *superstition* from which none of us is altogether free had given to solitude and darkness and silence only a more alluring interest and charm! I was unable to *comprehend* my folly, and losing in the conjecture the thing conjectured of, I fell asleep. And then I dreamed.

I was in a great city in a foreign land -- a city whose people were of my own race, with minor differences of speech and costume; yet precisely what these were I could not say; my sense of them was indistinct. The city was dominated by a great castle upon an overlooking height whose name I knew, but could not speak. I walked through many streets, some broad and straight with high, modern buildings, some narrow, gloomy, and *tortuous*, between the gables of quaint old houses whose *overhanging* stories, elaborately ornamented with carvings in wood and stone, almost met above my head.

I sought some one whom I had never seen, yet knew that I should recognise when found. My quest was not aimless and fortuitous; it had a definite method. I turned from one street into another without hesitation and threaded a *maze* of intricate passages, devoid of the fear of losing my way.

Presently I stopped before a low door in a plain stone house which might have been the dwelling of an artisan of the bette sort, and without announcing myself, entered. The room, rather sparely furnished, and lighted by a single window with small diamond-shaped panes, had but two occupants: a man and a woman. They took no notice of my intrusion, a circumstance which, in the manner of dreams, appeared entirely natural. They were not conversing; they sat apart, *unoccupied* and *sullen*.

Malign - *Vilify, baneful*
Indistinct - *Not clear*
Grasped - *To seize*
Muzzle - *Th mouth*
Tortuous - *Painful*
Maze - *Delusion*

The woman was young and rather stout, with fine large eyes and a certain grave beauty; my memory of her expression is *exceedingly* vivid, but in dreams one does not observe the details of faces. About her shoulders was a plaid shawl. The man was older, dark, with an evil face made more forbidding by a long scar extending from near the left temple diagonally downward into the black moustache; though in my dreams it seemed rather to haunt the face as a thing apart -- I can express it no otherwise -- than to belong to it. The moment that I found the man and woman I knew them to be husband and wife.

What followed, I remember indistinctly; all was confused and inconsistent -- made so, I think, by gleams of consciousness. It was as if two pictures, the scene of my dream, and my actual surroundings, had been blended, one *overlying* the other, until the former, gradually fading, disappeared, and I was broad awake in the deserted cabin, entirely and tranquilly conscious of my situation.

My foolish fear was gone, and opening my eyes I saw that my fire, not altogether burned out, had revived by the falling of a stick and was again lighting the room. I had probably slept only a few minutes, but my commonplace dream had somehow so strongly *impressed* me that I was no longer drowsy; and after a little while I rose, pushed the embers of my fire together, and lighting my pipe proceeded in a rather *ludicrously* methodical way to meditate upon my vision.

It would have puzzled me then to say in what respect it was worth attention. In the first moment of serious thought that I gave to the matter I recognised the city of my dream as Edinburgh, where I had never been; so if the dream was a memory it was a memory of pictures and description. The recognition somehow deeply impressed me; it was as if something in my mind insisted rebelliously against will and reason on the importance of all this. And that faculty, whatever it was, asserted also a control of my speech. 'Surely,' I said aloud, quite involuntarily, 'the MacGregors must have come here from Edinburgh.'

At the moment, neither the substance of this remark nor the fact of my making it surprised me in the least; it seemed entirely natural that I should know the name of my dreamfolk and something of their history. But the absurdity of it all soon dawned upon me: I laughed aloud, knocked the ashes from my pipe and again stretched myself upon my bed of boughs and grass, where I lay staring absently into my failing fire, with no further thought

---

Exceedingly - *To a very great degree*
Overlying - *To lie over*
Impressed - *To affect deeply*
Ludicrously - *Ridiculously*

of either my dream or my surroundings. Suddenly the single remaining flame *crouched* for a moment, then, springing upward, lifted itself clear of its embers and expired in air. The darkness was absolute.

At that instant -- almost, it seemed, before the gleam of the blaze had faded from my eyes --

there was a dull, dead sound, as of some heavy body falling upon the floor, which shook beneath me as I lay. I sprang to a sitting posture and groped at my side for my gun; my notion was that some wild beast had leaped in through the open window. While the *flims* structure was still shaking from the impact I heard the sound of blows, the *scuffli* of feet upon the floor and then -- it seemed to come from almost within reach of my hand, the sharp shrieking of a woman in mortal agony. So horrible a cry I had never heard nor *conceived*; it utterly unnerved me; I was conscious for a moment of nothing but my own terror! Fortunately my hand now found the weapon of which it was in search, and the familiar touch somewhat restored me. I leaped to my feet, straining my eyes to pierce the darkness. The violent sounds had ceased, but more terrible than these, I heard, at what seemed long intervals, the faint *intermitten* gasping of some living, dying thing!

As my eyes grew accustomed to the dim light of the coals in the fireplace, I saw first the shapes of the door and window looking blacker than the black of the walls. Next, the distinction between wall and floor became discernible, and at last I was sensible to the form and full expanse of the floor from end to end and side to side. Nothing was visible and the silence was unbroken.

With a hand that shook a little, the other still *grasping* my gun, I restored my fire and made a critical examination of the place. There was nowhere any sign that the cabin had been entered. My own tracks were visible in the dust covering the floor but there were no others. I relit my pipe, provided fresh fuel by ripping a thin board or two from the inside of the house -- I did not care to go into the darkness out of doors -- and passed the rest of the night smoking and thinking, and feeding my fire; not for added years of life would I have permitted that little flam to *expire* again.

Some years afterward I met in Sacramento a man named Morgan, to whom I had a note of introduction from a friend in San Francisco. Dining with him one evening at his home I observed various *'trophies'* upon the wall, indicating that he

Crouched - *To stoop or bend low*
Flimsy - *Weak*
Scuffl g - *To move in a hurry/confusion*
Conceived - *To form a notion*
Intermittent - *Stopping or ceasing for a time*

Best Stories of Ambrose Bierce

was fond of shooting. It turned out that he was, and in relating some of his feats he mentioned having been in the region of my adventure.

'Mr. Morgan,' I asked abruptly, 'do you know a place up there called Macarger's Gulch?'

'I have good reason to,' he replied; 'it was I who gave to the newspapers, last year, the accounts of the finding of the skeleton there."

I had not heard of it; the accounts had been published, it appeared, while I was absent in the East.

'By the way,' said Morgan, 'the name of the gulch is a *corruption*; it should have been called "MacGregor's." My dear,' he added, speaking to his wife, 'Mr. Elderson has upset his wine.'

That was hardly accurate -- I had simply dropped it, glass and all.

'There was an old *shanty* once in the gulch,' Morgan resumed when the ruin *wrought* by my awkwardness had been repaired, 'but just previously to my visit it had been blown down, or rather blown away, for its *debris* was scattered all about, the very floo being parted, plank from plank. Between two of the sleepers still in position I and my companion observed the remnant of a plaid shawl, and examining it found that it was wrapped about the shoulders of the body of a woman; of course but little remained besides the bones, partly covered with fragments of clothing, and brown dry skin. But we will spare Mrs. Morgan,' he added with a smile. The lady had indeed exhibited signs of *disgust* rather than sympathy.

'It is necessary to say, however,' he went on, 'that the skull was *fractured* in several places, as by blows of some blunt instrument; and that instrument itself -- a pick-handle, still stained with blood -- lay under the boards near by.'

Mr. Morgan turned to his wife. 'Pardon me, my dear,' he said with affected *solemnity*, 'for mentioning these disagreeable particulars, the natural though *regrettabl* incidents of a conjugal quarrel -- resulting, doubtless, from the luckless wife's *insubordination*.'

'I ought to be able to overlook it,' the lady replied with *composure*; 'you have so many times asked me to in those very words.'

I thought he seemed rather glad to go on with his story.

'From these and other circumstances,' he said, 'the coroner's jury found that the deceased, Janet MacGregor, came to her death

Expire - *To die*
Corruption - *Moral perversion*
Shanty - *Crudely built hut*
Wrought - *Worked, laboured*
Debris - *the remains or trash*
Fractured - *Th breaking of a bone or cartilage*

from blows *inflicte* by some person to the jury unknown; but it was added that the *evidence* pointed strongly to her husband, Thomas MacGregor, as the guilty person. But Thomas MacGregor has never been found nor heard of. It was learned that the couple came from Edinburgh, but not -- my dear, do you not observe that Mr. Elderson's bone-plate has water in it?'

I had deposited a chicken bone in my finger bo l.

'In a little cupboard I found a photograph of MacGregor, but it did not lead to his capture.'

'Will you let me see it?' I said.

The picture showed a dark man with an evil face made more *forbidding* by a long scar extending from near the temple diagonally downward into the black moustache.

'By the way, Mr. Elderson,' said my *affabl* host, 'may I know why you asked about "Macarger's Gulch"?'

'I lost a mule near there once,' I replied, 'and the mischance has -- has quite -- upset me.'

'My dear,' said Mr. Morgan, with the mechanical *intonation* of an *interpreter* translating, 'the loss of Mr. Elderson's mule has peppered his coffee.'

Food For Thought

Who was the deceased and how did her husband, Thomas Macgregor kill her? Do you think that the narrator, Mr. Elderson dreamt of Janet Macgregor and her husband when he spent that night in the lonely house or was it the ghost of Ms. Janet Macgregor? How did Elderson recognise the city of his dream as Edinburgh?

Inflic ed - *Afflicted*
Evidence - *Proof*
Forbidding - *Preventing*
Affable - *Cordial, friendly*
Intonation - *Changing patterns of the pitch of avoice*
Interpreter - *A person who translates orally*

The Moonlit Road
Ambrose Bierce

1. Statement of Joel Hetman, Jr.

I am the most unfortunate of men. Rich, respected, fairly well educated and of sound health -- with many other advantages usually valued by those having them and *coveted* by those who have them not -- I sometimes think that I should be less unhappy if they had been denied me, for then the contrast between my outer and my inner life would not be *continually* demanding a painful attention. In the stress of *privation* and the need of effort I might sometimes forget the sombre secret ever baffling the conjecture that it compels

I am the only child of Joel and Julia Hetman. The one was a well-to-do country gentleman, the other a beautiful and accomplished woman to whom he was passionately attached with what I now know to have been a jealous and *exacting* devotion. The family home was a few miles from Nashville, Tennessee, a large, irregularly built dwelling of no particular order of architecture, a little way off the road, in a park of trees and shrubbery.

At the time of which I write I was nineteen years old, a student at Yale. One day I received a telegram from my father of such urgency that in compliance with its unexplained demand I left at once for home. At the railway station in Nashville a distant relative awaited me to apprise me of the reason for my recall: my mother had been barbarously murdered -- why and by whom none could *conjecture*, but the circumstances were these.

My father had gone to Nashville, intending to return the next afternoon. Something prevented his *accomplishing* the business in hand, so he returned on the same night, arriving just before the dawn. In his testimony before the coroner he explained that having no latchkey and not caring to disturb the sleeping servants, he had, with no clearly defined intention, gone round to the rear of the house. As he turned an angle of the building, he heard a sound as of a door gently closed, and saw in the darkness, *indistinctly*, the figure of a man, which instantly disappeared among the trees of the lawn. A hasty *pursuit* and brief search of the grounds in the belief that the trespasser was some one secretly visiting a servant proving

Coveted - *Wrongful desire*
Exacting - *Rigid or severe in demands*
Conjecture - *Guess, speculation*
Accomplishing - *Succeeding*
Pursuit - *Chase, hunt*

fruitless, he entered at the unlocked door and mounted the stairs to my mother's chamber. Its door was open, and stepping into black darkness he fell headlong over some heavy object on the floor. I may spare myself the details; it was my poor mother, dead of **strangulation** by human hands!

Nothing had been taken from the house, the servants had heard no sound, and excepting those terrible finger-marks upon the dead woman's throat -- dear God! that I might forget them! -- no trace of the *assassin* was ever found.

I gave up my studies and remained with my father, who, naturally, was greatly changed. Always of a sedate, **taciturn disposition**, he now fell into so deep a dejection that nothing could hold his attention, yet anything -- a footfall, the sudden closing of a door -- aroused in him a fitful interest; one might have called it an **apprehension**. At any small surprise of the senses he would start visibly and sometimes turn pale, then relapse into a melancholy apathy deeper than before. I suppose he was what is called a 'nervous wreck.' As to me, I was younger then than now -- there is much in that. Youth is Gilead, in which is balm for every wound. Ah, that I might again dwell in that enchanted land! Unacquainted with grief, I knew not how to appraise my **bereavement**; I could not rightly estimate the strength of the stroke.

One night, a few months after the dreadful event, my father and I walked home from the city. The full moon was about three hours above the eastern horizon; the entire countryside had the **solemn** stillness of a summer night; our footfalls and the ceaseless song of the katydids were the only sound, aloof. Black shadows of bordering trees lay athwart the road, which, in the short reaches between, gleamed a ghostly white. As we approached the gate to our dwelling, whose front was in shadow, and in which no light shone, my father suddenly stopped and **clutched** my arm, saying, hardly above his breath:

'God! God! what is that?'

'I hear nothing,' I replied.

'But see -- see!' he said, pointing along the road, directly ahead.

I said: 'Nothing is there. Come, father, let us go in -- you are ill.'

He had released my arm and was standing rigid and motionless in the centre of the **illuminated** roadway, staring like

Assassin - *Murderer*
Taciturn - *Stern*
Disposition - *Final settlement*
Apprehension - *Opinion*
Bereavement - *A period of mourning*
Illuminated - *Lighted*

one bereft of sense. His face in the moonlight showed a pallor and fixity inexpressibly *distressing*. I pulled gently at his sleeve, but he had forgotten my existence. Presently he began to retire backward, step by step, never for an instant removing his eyes from what he saw, or thought he saw. I turned half round to follow, but stood irresolute. I do not recall any feeling of fear, unless a sudden chill was its physical *manifestation*. It seemed as if an icy wind had touched my face and enfolded my body from head to foot; I could feel the stir of it in my hair.

At that moment my attention was drawn to a light that suddenly streamed from an upper window of the house: one of the servants, awakened by what mysterious *premonition* of evil who can say, and in obedience to an impulse that she was never able to name, had lit a lamp. When I turned to look for my father he was gone, and in all the years that have passed no whisper of his fate has come across the borderland of conjecture from the realm of the unknown.

2. Statement of Caspar Grattan

To-day I am said to live, to-morrow, here in this room, will lie a senseless shape of clay that all too long was I. If anyone lift the cloth from the face of that unpleasant thing it will be in *gratifiction* of a mere morbid curiosity. Some, doubtless, will go further and inquire, 'Who was he?' In this writing I supply the only answer that I am able to make -- Caspar Grattan. Surely, that should be enough. The name has served my small need for more than twenty years of a life of unknown length. True, I gave it to myself, but lacking another I had the right. In this world one must have a name; it prevents confusion, even when it does not establish identity. Some, though, are known by numbers, which also seem inadequate distinctions.

One day, for illustration, I was passing along a street of a city, far from here, when I met two men in uniform, one of whom, half pausing and looking curiously into my face, said to his companion, 'That man looks like 767.' Something in the number seemed familiar and horrible. Moved by an uncontrollable impulse, I sprang into a side street and ran until I fell *exhausted* in a countrylane.

I have never forgotten that number, and always it comes to memory attended by *gibbering obscenity, peals* of joyless

Distressing - *Great pain*
Manifestation - *Display*
Premonition - *Forewarning*
Gratifi ation - *Reward*

laughter, the clang of iron doors. So I say a name, even if self-bestowed, is better than a number. In the register of the potte's field I shall soon ha e both. What wealth!

Of him who shall find this paper I must beg a little consideration. It is not the history of my life; the knowledge to write that is denied me. This is only a record of broken and apparently unrelated memories, some of them as distinct and sequent as brilliant beads upon a thread, others remote and strange, having the character of crimson dreams with interspaces blank and black -- witch-fires glowing still and red in a great *desolation*.

Standing upon the shore of eternity, I turn for a last look landward over the course by which I came. There are twenty years of footprints fairly distinct, the impressions of bleeding feet. They lead through poverty and pain, devious and unsure, as of one *staggering* beneath a burden -- Remote, unfriended, melancholy, slow.

Ah, the poet's prophecy of Me -- how admirable, how dreadfully admirable!

Backward beyond the beginning of this via *dolorosa* -- this epic of suffering with episodes of sin -- I see nothing clearly; it comes out of a cloud. I know that it spans only twenty years, yet I am an old man.

One does not remember one's birth -- one has to be told. But with me it was different; life came to me full-handed and dowered me with all my faculties and powers. Of a previous existence I know no more than others, for all have *stammering intimations* that may be memories and may be dreams. I know only that my first consciousness was of maturity in body and mind -- a consciousness accepted without surprise or conjecture. I merely found myself walking in a forest, half-clad, footsore, *unutterabl weary* and hungry. Seeing a farmhouse, I approached and asked for food, which was given me by one who inquired my name. I did not know, yet knew that all had names. Greatly embarrassed, I retreated, and night coming on, lay down in the forest and slept.

The next day I entered a large town which I shall not name. Nor shall I recount further incidents of the life that is now to end -- a life of wandering, always and everywhere haunted by an *overmastering* sense of crime in punishment of wrong and of terror in punishment of crime. Let me see if I can reduce it to *narrative*.

Dolorosa - *Th sorrowful mother of Lord Christ*
Stammering - *Hesitating voice*
Intimidations - *Fill with fear*
Weary - *Tired*

I seem once to have lived near a great city, a prosperous planter, married to a woman whom I loved and distrusted. We had, it sometimes seems, one child, a youth of brilliant parts and promise. He is at all times a vague figure, never clearly drawn, frequently altogether out of the picture.

One luckless evening it occurred to me to test my wife's fidelity in a vulgar, commonplace way familiar to everyone who has acquaintance with the literature of fact and fiction. I went to the city, telling my wife that I should be absent until the following afternoon. But I returned before ***daybreak*** and went to the rear of the house, purposing to enter by a door with which I had secretly so tampered that it would seem to lock, yet not actually fasten. As I approached it, I heard it gently open and close, and saw a man steal away into the darkness. With murder in my heart, I sprang after him, but he had vanished without even the bad luck of identification. Sometimes now I cannot even ***persuade*** myself that it was a human being.

Crazed with jealousy and rage, blind and bestial with all the elemental passions of insulted manhood, I entered the house and sprang up the stairs to the door of my wife's chamber. It was closed, but having tampered with its lock also, I easily entered, and despite the black darkness soon stood by the side of her bed. My groping hands told me that although ***disarranged*** it was unoccupied.

'She is below,' I thought, 'and terrified by my entrance has ***evaded*** me in the darkness of the hall.' With the purpose of seeking her I turned to leave the room, but took a wrong direction -- the right one! My foot struck her, cowering in a corner of the room. Instantly my hands were at her throat, stifling a shriek, my knees were upon her struggling body; and there in the darkness, without a word of accusation or reproach, I strangled her till she died! There ends the dream. I have related it in the past tense, but the present would be the fitte form, for again and again the sombre tragedy ***re-enacts*** itself in my consciousness -- over and over I lay the plan, I suffer the ***confirmatio*** , I redress the wrong. Then all is blank; and afterward the rains beat against the ***grimy*** windowpanes, or the snows fall upon my scant attire, the wheels rattle in the ***squalid*** streets where my life lies in poverty and mean employment. If there is ever sunshine I do not recall it; if there are birds they do not sing.

Daybreak - *The first appearance of day light*
Persuade - *To urge, convince*
Evaded - *To escape*
Re-enacts - *To make into an act*
Grimy - *Dirty, squalid*

There is another dream, another vision of the night. I stand among the shadows in a moonlit road. I am aware of another presence, but whose I cannot rightly determine. In the shadow of a great dwelling I catch the gleam of white garments; then the figure of a woman confronts me in the road -- my murdered wife! There is death in the face; there are marks upon the throat. The eyes are fixed on mine with an infinite gravity which is not reproach, nor hate, nor menace, nor anything less terrible than recognition. Before this awful apparition I retreat in terror -- a terror that is upon me as I write. I can no longer rightly shape the words. See! they -- Now I am calm, but truly there is no more to tell: the incident ends where it began -- in darkness and in doubt.

Yes, I am again in control of myself: 'the captain of my soul.' But that is not respite; it is another stage and phase of *expiation*. My penance, constant in degree, is mutable in kind: one of its variants is *tranquillity*. After all, it is only a life-sentence. 'To Hell for life' -- that is a foolish penalty: the culprit chooses the duration of his punishment. To-day my term *expires*.

To each and all, the peace that was not mine.

3. Statement of the Late Julia Hetman, through the Medium Bayrolles

I had retired early and fallen almost immediately into a peaceful sleep, from which I awoke with that indefinable sense of peril which is, I think, a common experience in that other, earlier life. Of its unmeaning character, too, I was entirely persuaded, yet that did not banish it. My husband, Joel Hetman, was away from home; the servants slept in another part of the house. But these were familiar conditions; they had never before distressed me. Nevertheless, the strange terror grew so insupportable that conquering my *reluctance* to move I sat up and lit the lamp at my bedside. Contrary to my expectation this gave me no relief; the light seemed rather an added danger, for I reflected that it would shine out under the door, *disclosing* my presence to whatever evil thing might lurk outside. You that are still in the flesh, subject to horrors of the imagination, think what a monstrous fear that must be which seeks in darkness security from malevolent existences of the night. That is to spring to close quarters with an unseen enemy -- the strategy of despair!

Extinguishing the lamp I pulled the bedclothing about my head and lay trembling and silent, unable to shriek, forgetful to

Squalid - *Foul and repulsive*
Expiation - *Faithful, loyal*
Tranquillity - *Calm, quietude*
Expires - *To come to an end, terminate*
Reluctance - *Unwillingness*

pray. In this *pitiable* state I must have lain for what you call hours -- with us there are no hours, there is no time.

At last it came -- a soft, irregular sound of footfalls on the stairs! They were slow, hesitant, uncertain, as of something that did not see its way; to my disordered reason all the more terrifying for that, as the approach of some blind and mindless malevolence to which is no appeal. I even thought that I must have left the hall lamp burning and the groping of this creature proved it a monster of the night. This was foolish and inconsistent with my previous dread of the light, but what would you have? Fear has no brains; it is an idiot. The *dismal* witness that it bears and the cowardly counsel that it whispers are unrelated. We know this well, we who have passed into the Realm of Terror, who skulk in eternal dusk among the scenes of our former lives, invisible even to ourselves, and one another, yet hiding forlorn in lonely places; yearning for speech with our loved ones, yet dumb, and as fearful of them as they of us. Sometimes the disability is removed, the law suspended: by the deathless power of love or hate we break the spell -- we are seen by those whom we would warn, *console*, or punish. What form we seem to them to bear we know not; we know only that we terrify even those whom we most wish to comfort, and from whom we most crave tenderness and sympathy.

Forgive, I pray you, this *inconsequent digression* by what was once a woman. You who consult us in this imperfect way -- you do not understand. You ask foolish questions about things unknown and things *forbidden*. Much that we know and could impart in our speech is meaningless in yours. We must communicate with you through a stammering intelligence in that small fraction of our language that you yourselves can speak. You think that we are of another world. No, we have knowledge of no world but yours, though for us it holds no sunlight, no warmth, no music, no laughter, no song of birds, nor any *companionship*. O God! what a thing it is to be a ghost, cowering and shivering in an altered world, a prey to *apprehension* and despair!

No, I did not die of fright: the Thing turned and went away. I heard it go down the stairs, hurriedly, I thought, as if itself in sudden fear. Then I rose to call for help. Hardly had my shaking hand found the door-knob when -- merciful heaven! -- I heard it returning. Its footfalls as it remounted the stairs were rapid, heavy and loud; they shook the house. I fled to an angle of the

Disclosing - *Reveal*
Extinguishing - *To put out a fire, light, etc.*
Dismal - *Gloomy*
Console - *Solace*
Digression - *Deviation*
Forbidden - *Prohibited*

wall and crouched upon the floor. I tried to pray. I tried to call the name of my dear husband. Then I heard the door thrown open. There was an interval of unconsciousness, and when I revived I felt a strangling clutch upon my throat -- felt my arms *feebly* beating against something that bore me backward -- felt my tongue *thrusting* itself from between my teeth! And then I passed into this life.

No, I have no knowledge of what it was. The sum of what we knew at death is the measure of what we know afterward of all that went before. Of this existence we know many things, but no new light falls upon any page of that; in memory is written all of it that we can read. Here are no heights of truth overlooking the confused landscape of that dubitable domain. We still dwell in the Valley of the Shadow, *lurk* in its desolate places, peering from brambles and thickets at its mad, malign inhabitants. How should we have new knowledge of that fading past?

What I am about to relate happened on a night. We know when it is night, for then you retire to your houses and we can venture from our places of *concealment* to move unafraid about our old homes, to look in at the windows, even to enter and gaze upon your faces as you sleep. I had lingered long near the dwelling where I had been so cruelly changed to what I am, as we do while any that we love or hate remain. Vainly I had sought some method of *manifestation,* some way to make my continued existence and my great love and poignant pity understood by my husband and son. Always if they slept they would wake, or if in my desperation I dared approach them when they were awake, would turn toward me the terrible eyes of the living, frightening me by the glances that I sought from the purpose that I held.

On this night I had searched for them without success, fearing to find them; they were nowhere in the house, nor about the moonlit dawn. For, although the sun is lost to us for ever, the moon, full-orbed or slender, remains to us. Sometimes it shines by night, sometimes by day, but always it rises and sets, as in that other life.

I left the lawn and moved in the white light and silence along the road, aimless and sorrowing. Suddenly I heard the voice of my poor husband in *exclamations* of astonishment, with that of my son in reassurance and dissuasion; and there by the shadow of a group of trees they stood -- near, so near! Their faces were toward me, the eyes of the elder man fixed upon mine. He saw

Feebly - *Physically weak*
Th usting - *Enforcing*
Lurk - *To wait or hid secretly*
Concealment - *To keep secret*
Manifestation - *Displaying*

me -- at last, at last, he saw me! In the consciousness of that, my terror fled as a cruel dream. The death-spell was broken: Love had conquered Law! Mad with *exultation* I shouted -- I must have shouted,' He sees, he sees: he will understand!' Then, controlling myself, I moved forward, smiling and consciously beautiful, to offer myself to his arms, to comfort him with *endearments*, and, with my son's hand in mine, to speak words that should restore the broken bonds between the living and the dead.

Alas! alas! his face went white with fear, his eyes were as those of a hunted animal. He backed away from me, as I advanced, and at last turned and fled into the wood -- *whither*, it is not given to me to know.

To my poor boy, left doubly desolate, I have never been able to impart a sense of my presence. Soon he, too, must pass to this Life Invisible and be lost to me for ever.

Food For Thought

Julia Hetman's husband suspected his wife of infidelity. Do you think that this was the main reason for him to kill her, or do you think that her lover killed her? Why did Julia's husband disappear into the moonlit night when he heard strange noises while walking with his son?

Impart - *Disclose, relate*
Desolate - *Deprived, solitary*
Exultation - *Triumphant joy*
Endearments - *Affectionate utt rance*
Whither - *Where*

The Haunted Valley
~ Ambrose Bierce

I. How Trees Are Felled in China

A half-mile north from Jo. Dunfer's, on the road from Hutton's to Mexican Hill, the highway dips into a sunless ravine which opens out on either hand in a half-*confidentia* manner, as if it had a secret to impart at some more convenient season. I never used to ride through it without looking first to the one side and then to the other, to see if the time had arrived for the *revelation*. If I saw nothing -- and I never did see anything -- there was no feeling of disappointment, for I knew the disclosure was merely withheld temporarily for some good reason which I had no right to question. That I should one day be taken into full confidence I no more doubted than I doubted the existence of Jo. Dunfer himself, through whose premises the *ravine* ran.

It was said that Jo. had once undertaken to erect a cabin in some remote part of it, but for some reason had abandoned the enterprise and constructed his present *hermaphrodite* habitation, half residence and half groggery, at the roadside, upon an extreme corner of his estate; as far away as possible, as if on purpose to show how radically he had changed his mind.

This Jo. Dunfer -- or, as he was familiarly known in the neighbourhood, Whisky Jo. -- was a very important personage in those parts. He was apparently about forty years of age, a long, shock-headed fellow, with a corded face, a gnarled arm and a knotty hand like a bunch of prison-keys. He was a hairy man, with a stoop in his walk, like that of one who is about to spring upon something and rend it.

Next to the peculiarity to which he owed his local appellation, Mr. Dunfer's most obvious characteristic was a deep-seated antipathy to the Chinese. I saw him once in a *towering* rage because one of his herdsmen had permitted a travel-heated Asian to slake his thirst at the horse-trough in front of the saloon end of Jo.'s establishment. I *ventured* faintly to *remonstrate* with Jo. for his unchristian spirit, but he merely explained that there was nothing about Chinamen in the

Confid ntial - *Private*
Revelation - *Disclosure*
Ravine - *A deep narrow steep sided valley*
hermaphrodite *- Combining two opposite qualities*
Remonstrate - *To plead in protest*

New Testament, and strode away to wreak his displeasure upon his dog, which also, I suppose, the inspired scribes had overlooked.

Some days afterward, finding him sitting alone in his barroom, I *cautiously* approached the subject, when, greatly to my relief, the habitual austerity of his expression visibly softened into something that I took for condescension.

'You young Easterners,' he said, 'are a mile-and-a-half too good for this country, and you don't catch on to our play. People who don't know a Chileno from a Kanaka can affor to hang out liberal ideas about Chinese *immigration*, but a fellow that has to fight for his bone with a lot of mongrel coolies hasn't any time for foolishness.'

This long consumer, who had probably never done an honest day's work in his life, sprung the lid of a Chinese tobacco-box and with thumb and forefinger forked out a wad like a small haycock. Holding this *reinforcement* within supporting distance he fired a ay with renewed confidence

'They're a flight of devouring locusts, and they're going for everything green in this God blest land, if you want to know.'

Here he pushed his reserve into the breach and when his gabble-gear was again *disengaged* resumed his uplifting discourse.

'I had one of them on this ranch fi e years ago, and I'll tell you about it, so that you can see the *nub* of this whole question. I didn't pan out particularly well those days -- drank more whisky than was prescribed for me and didn't seem to care for my duty as a patriotic American citizen; so I took that pagan in, as a kind of cook. But when I got religion over at the Hill and they talked of running me for the Legislature it was given to me to see the light. But what was I to do? If I gave him the go somebody else would take him, and mightn't treat him white. What was I to do? What would any good Christian do, especially one new to the trade and full to the neck with the brotherhood of Man and the fatherhood of God?'

Jo. paused for a reply, with an expression of *unstable* satisfaction, as of one who has solved a problem by a *distrusted* method. Presently he rose and swallowed a glass of whisky from a full bottle on the counter, then *resumed* his story.

'Besides, he didn't count for much -- didn't know anything and gave himself airs. They all do that. I said him nay, but he

Cautiously - *Carefully*
Immigration - *Th movement of non-active people into a country to settle*
Reinforcement - *To give added strength or support*
Nub - *A knob*
Resumed - *To begin again*
Muled - *To use roughly*

muled it through on that line while he lasted; but after turning the other cheek seventy and seven times I doctored the dice so that he didn't last for ever. And I'm almighty glad I had the sand to do it.'

Jo.'s gladness, which somehow did not impress me, was duly and *ostentatiously* celebrated at the bottle.

'About fi e years ago I started in to stick up a shack. That was before this one was built, and I put it in another place. I set Ah Wee and a little *cuss* named Gopher to cutting the timber. Of course I didn't expect Ah Wee to help much, for he had a face like a day in June and big black eyes -- I guess maybe they were the damn'dest eyes in this neck o' woods.'

While delivering this trenchant thrust at common sense Mr. Dunfer absently regarded a knot-hole in the thin board partition separating the bar from the living-room, as if that were one of the eyes whose size and colour had incapacitated his servant for good service.

'Now you Eastern galoots won't believe anything against the yellow devils,' he suddenly flamed out with an appearance of *earnestness* not altogether convincing, 'but I tell you that Chink was the perversest scoundrel outside San Francisco. The miserable pig-tail Mongolian went to hewing away at the *saplings* all round the stems, like a worm o' the dust gnawing a radish. I pointed out his error as patiently as I knew how, and showed him how to cut them on two sides, so as to make them fall right; but no sooner would I turn my back on him, like this' -- and he turned it on me, *amplifying* the illustration by taking some more liquor -- 'than he was at it again. It was just this way: while I looked at him so' -- regarding me rather *unsteadily* and with evident complexity of vision -- ' he was all right; but when I looked away, so' -- taking a long pull at the bottle -- 'he defied me. Then I'd gaze at him reproachfully, so, and butter wouldn't ha e melted in his mouth.'

Doubtless Mr. Dunfer honestly intended the look that he fixed upon me to be merely *reproachful*, but it was singularly fit to arouse the gravest apprehension in any unarmed person incurring it; and as I had lost all interest in his pointless and interminable narrative, I rose to go. Before I had fairly risen, he had again turned to the counter, and with a barely audible 'so,' had emptied the bottle at a gulp.

Heavens! what a yell! It was like a Titan in his last, strong agony. Jo. staggered back after emitting it, as a cannon *recoils*

Ostentatiously - *Showy, pretentious*
Cuss - *Cusse, swear*
Earnestness - *Truthfulness, sincerity*
Saplings - *Young trees*
Amplifying - *To make larger or greater*
Reproachful - *Disgraceful*
Recoils - *To draw back, shrink*

from its own thunder, and then dropped into his chair, as if he had been 'knocked in the head' like a beef -- his eyes drawn sidewise toward the wall, with a stare of terror. Looking in the same direction, I saw that the *knothole* in the wall had indeed become a human eye -- a full, black eye, that glared into my own with an entire lack of expression more awful than the most devilish glitter. I think I must have covered my face with my hands to shut out the horrible illusion, if such it was, and Jo.'s little white man-of-all-work coming into the room broke the spell, and I walked out of the house with a sort of dazed fear that delirium tremens might be *infectious*. My horse was hitched at the watering-trough, and untying him I mounted and gave him his head, too much troubled in mind to note whither he took me.

I did not know what to think of all this, and like everyone who does not know what to think I thought a great deal, and to little purpose. The only reflection that seemed at all satisfactory was, that on the morrow I should be some miles away, with a strong *probability* of never returning. A sudden coolness brought me out of my abstraction, and looking up I found myself entering the deep shadows of the ravine. The day was stifling; and this *transition* from the pitiless, visible heat of the parched fields to the cool gloom, heavy with pungency of cedars and vocal with twittering of the birds that had been driven to its leafy asylum, was exquisitely refreshing. I looked for my mystery, as usual, but not finding the ravine in a communicative mood, *dismounted*, led my sweating animal into the undergrowth, tied him securely to a tree and sat down upon a rock to meditate.

I began bravely by analysing my pet superstition about the place. Having resolved it into its constituent elements I arranged them in convenient troops and squadrons, and collecting all the forces of my logic bore down upon them from *impregnable* premises with the thunder of irresistible conclusions and a great noise of chariots and general intellectual shouting. Then, when my big mental guns had overturned all opposition, and were growling almost inaudibly away on the horizon of pure *speculation*, the routed enemy *straggled* in upon their rear, massed silently into a solid *phalanx*, and captured me, bag and baggage. An indefiable dread came upon me. I rose to shake it off, and began threading the narrow dell by an old, grass-grown cow-path

---

Knothole - *A hole in a board*
Transition - *Change*
Dismounted - *To get off, light*
Impregnable - *Invulnerable*
Straggled - *To wander*
Phalanx - *Any body of troops*

that seemed to flow along the bottom, as a substitute for the brook that Nature had neglected to provide.

The trees among which the path *straggled* were ordinary, well-behaved plants, a trifle perverted as to trunk and eccentric as to bough, but with nothing unearthly in their general aspect. A few loose boulders, which had detached themselves from the sides of the depression to set up an independent existence at the bottom, had dammed up the pathway, here and there, but their stony repose had nothing in it of the stillness of death. There was a kind of death-chamber hush in the valley, it is true, and a mysterious whisper above: the wind was just fingerin the tops of the trees -- that was all.

I had not thought of connecting Jo. Dunfer's drunken narrative with what I now sought, and only when I came into a clear space and stumbled over the level trunks of some small trees did I have the revelation. This was the site of the abandoned 'shack.' The discovery was verified by noting that some of the rotting stumps were hacked all round, in a most unwoodman-like way, while others were cut straight across, and the butt ends of the corresponding trunks had the blunt wedge-form given by the axe of a master.

The opening among the trees was not more than thirty paces across. At one side was a little knoll-a natural *hillock*, bare of *shrubbery* but covered with wild grass, and on this, standing out of the grass, the *headstone* of a grave!

I do not remember that I felt anything like surprise at this discovery. I viewed that lonely grave with something of the feeling that Columbus must have had when he saw the hills and headlands of the new world. Before approaching it I leisurely completed my survey of the surroundings. I was even guilty of the affectation of winding my watch at that unusual hour, and with needless care and *deliberation*. Then I approached my mystery.

The grave -- a rather short one -- was in somewhat better repair than was consistent with its obvious age and isolation, and my eyes, I dare say, widened a trifle at a clump of unmistakable garden flo ers showing evidence of recent watering. The stone had clearly enough done duty once as a doorstep. In its front was carved, or rather dug, an *inscription*. It read thus:

AH WEE -- CHINAMAN.
Age unknown. Worked for Jo. Dunfer.

Hillock - *A small hill*
Shrubbery - *A planting of shrubs*
Headstone - *A memorial stone*
Deliberation - *Careful consideration*
Inscription - *Words engraved on rock, metal*

This monument is erected by him to keep the Chink's memory green. Likewise as a warning to **Celestials** not to take on airs. Devil take 'em! She Was a Good Egg.

I cannot adequately relate my astonishment at this uncommon inscription! The meagre but sufficien identification of the deceased; the *impudent candour* of *confession*; the brutal anathema; the ludicrous change of sex and sentiment -- all marked this record as the work of one who must have been at least as much demented as bereaved. I felt that any further disclosure would be a paltry *anti-climax*, and with an unconscious regard for dramatic effect turned squarely about and walked away. Nor did I return to that part of the county for four years.

II. Who Drives Sane Oxen Should Himself be Sane

'Gee-up, there, old Fuddy-Duddy!'

This unique adjuration came from the lips of a queer littl man perched upon a wagonful of firewood, behind a brace of oxen that were hauling it easily along with a simulation of mighty effort which had evidently not *imposed* on their lord and master. As that gentleman happened at the moment to be staring me squarely in the face as I stood by the roadside it was not altogether clear whether he was addressing me or his beasts; nor could I say if they were named Fuddy and Duddy and were both subjects of the *imperative* mood 'to gee-up.' Anyhow the command produced no effect on us, and the queer little man removed his eyes from mine long enough to spear Fuddy and Duddy alternately with a long pole, remarking, quietly but with feeling: 'Dern your skin,' as if they enjoyed that *integument* in common. Observing that my request for a ride took no attention, and finding myself falling slowly *astern*, I placed one foot upon the inner circumference of a hind wheel and was slowly elevated to the level of the hub, whence I boarded the concern, sans ceremonie, and scrambling forward seated myself beside the driver -- who took no notice of me until he had administered another indiscriminate castigation to his cattle, accompanied with the advice to 'buckle down, you derned Incapable!' Then, the master of the outfit (or rather the former master, for I could not suppress a *whimsical* feeling that the entire establishment was my lawful prize) trained his big, black eyes upon me with an expression strangely, and somewhat unpleasantly, familiar,

Astern - In a backward direction
Whimsical - Unpredictable
Celestials - Heavenly
Impudent - Insulting, rude
Candour - The state of being frank
Imperative - Absolutely necessary

laid down his rod -- which neither blossomed nor turned into a serpent, as I half expected -- folded his arms, and gravely demanded, 'W'at did you do to W'isky?'

My natural reply would have been that I drank it, but there was something about the query that suggested a hidden significance, and something about the man that did not invite a shallow *jest*. And so, having no other answer ready, I merely held my tongue, but felt as if I were resting under an imputation of guilt, and that my silence was being *construed* into a confession.

Just then a cold shadow fell upon my cheek, and caused me to look up. We were descending into my ravine! I cannot describe the sensation that came upon me: I had not seen it since it *unbosomed* itself four years before, and now I felt like one to whom a friend has made some sorrowing confession of crime long past, and who has basely deserted him in *consequence*. The old memories of Jo. Dunfer, his fragmentary revelation, and the unsatisfying explanatory note by the headstone, came back with singular *distinctness*. I wondered what had become of Jo., and -- I turned sharply around and asked my prisoner. He was intently watching his cattle, and without withdrawing his eyes replied:

'Gee-up, old Terrapin! He lies aside of Ah Wee up the gulch. Like to see it? They always come back to the spot -- I've been expectin' you. H-woa!'

At the enunciation of the aspirate, Fuddy-Duddy, the incapable *terrapin*, came to a dead halt, and before the vowel had died away up the ravine had folded up all his eight legs and lain down in the dusty road, regardless of the effect upon his derned skin. The queer little man slid off his seat to the ground and started up the dell without deigning to look back to see if I was following. But I was.

It was about the same season of the year, and at near the same hour of the day, of my last visit. The jays clamoured loudly, and the trees whispered darkly, as before; and I somehow traced in the two sounds a fanciful *analogy* to the open *boastfulness* of Mr. Jo. Dunfer's mouth and the mysterious reticence of his manner, and to the mingled *hardihood* and tenderness of his sole literary production -- the epitaph. All things in the valley seemed unchanged, excepting the cowpath, which was almost wholly overgrown with weeds. When

Jest - *A witty remark*
Construed - *Explain, interpret*
Terrapin - *Water tortoise*
Boastfulness - *Pride*
Analogy - *Similarity*

we came out into the 'clearing,' however, there was change enough. Among the stumps and trunks of the fallen saplings, those that had been hacked 'China fashion' were no longer distinguishable from those that were cut "Melican way.' It was as if the Old-World barbarism and the New-World civilization had reconciled their differences by the arbitration of an impartial decay -- as is the way of civilizations. The *knoll* was there, but the Hunnish brambles had overrun and all but obliterated its effete grasses; and the patrician garden-violet had capitulated to his plebeian brother -- perhaps had merely *reverted* to his original type. Another grave -- a long, robust mound -- had been made beside the first, which seemed to shrink from the comparison; and in the shadow of a new headstone the old one lay prostrate, with its marvellous inscription illegible by accumulation of leaves and soil. In point of literary merit the new was inferior to the old -- was even repulsive in its terse and s*avage jocularity*:

JO. DUNFER. DONE FOR

I turned from it with indifference, and brushing away the leaves from the tablet of the dead pagan restored to light the *mocking* words which, fresh from their long neglect, seemed to have a certain pathos. My guide, too, appeared to take on an added seriousness as he read it, and I fancied that I could detect beneath his whimsical manner something of *manliness*, almost of dignity. But while I looked at him his former aspect, so subtly unhuman, so *tantalizingly* familiar, crept back into his big eyes, repellent and attracti e. I resolved to make an end of the mystery if possible.

'My friend,' I said, pointing to the smaller grave, 'did Jo. Dunfer murder that Chinaman?'

He was *leaning* against a tree and looking across the open space into the top of another, or into the blue sky beyond. He neither withdrew his eyes, nor altered his posture as he slowly replied:

'No, sir; he *justifiably homicide* him.'

'Then he really did kill him.'

'Kill 'im? I should say he did, rather. Doesn't everybody know that? Didn't he stan' up before the coroner's jury and confess it? And didn't they find a verdict of "Came to 'is death by a *wholesome* Christian sentiment workin' in the Caucasian

Knoll - *A small rounded hill*
Revered - *Respected*
Savage - *Wild*
Jocularity - *Humorously*
Tantalizing - *Provoking*

breast"? An' didn't the church at the Hill turn W'isky down for it? And didn't the *sovereign* people elect him Justice of the Peace to get even on the *gospellers*? I don't know where you were brought up.'

'But did Jo. do that because the Chinaman did not, or would not, learn to cut down trees like a white man? '

'Sure! -- it stan's so on the record, which makes it true an' legal. My knowin' better doesn't make any difference with legal truth; it wasn't my funeral and I wasn't invited to deliver an *oration*. But the fact is, W'isky was jealous o' me' -- and the little wretch actually swelled out like a turkeycock and made a pretence of adjusting an imaginary neck-tie, noting the effect in the palm of his hand, held up before him to represent a mirror.

'Jealous of you!' I repeated with ill-mannered astonishment.

'That's what I said. Why not? -- don't I look all right?'

He assumed a mocking attitude of studied grace, and *twitched* the wrinkles out of his threadbare waistcoat. Then, suddenly dropping his voice to a low pitch of singular sweetness, he continued:

'W'isky thought a lot o' that Chink; nobody but me knew how 'e doted on 'im. Couldn't bear 'im out of 'is sight, the derned protoplasm! And w'en 'e came down to this clearin' one day an' found 'im an' me neglectin' our work -- 'im asleep an' me grapplin' a *tarantula* out of 'is sleeve -- W'isky laid hold of my axe and let us have it, good an' hard! I dodged just then, for the spider bit me, but Ah Wee got it bad in the side an' tumbled about like anything. W'isky was just weighin' me out one w'en 'e saw the spider fastened on my finger; then 'e knew 'e'd make a jackass of 'imself. 'E threw away the axe and got down on 'is knees alongside of Ah Wee, who gave a last little kick and opened 'is eyes -- 'e had eyes like mine -- an' puttin' up 'is hands drew down W'isky's ugly head and held it there w'ile 'e stayed. That wasn't long, for a tremblin' ran through 'im and 'e gave a bit of a moan an' beat the game.'

During the progress of the story the narrator had become *transfigure* . The comic, or rather, the sardonic element was all out of him, and as he painted that strange scene it was with difficulty that I kept my composure. And this *consummate* actor had somehow so managed me that the sympathy due to

Sovereign - *Supreme*
Gspellers - *A preacher of the Christian gospel*
Tarantula - *Larger hairy tropical spiders*
Transfigured - *Transformed*
Consummate - *Fulfill*

his dramatis personae was given to himself. I stepped forward to grasp his hand, when suddenly a broad *grin* danced across his face and with a light, mocking laugh he continued:

'W'en W'isky got 'is nut out o' that 'e was a sight to see! All 'is fine clothes -- 'e dressed mighty blindin' those days -- were spoiled everlastin'! 'Is hair was tousled and 'is face -- what I could see of it -- was whiter than the ace of lilies. 'E stared once at me, and looked away as if I didn't count; an' then there were shootin' pains chasin' one another from my bitten finger into my head, and it was Gopher to the dark. That's why I wasn't at the inquest.'

'But why did you hold your tongue afterward?' I asked.

'It's that kind of tongue,' he replied, and not another word would he say about it.

'After that W'isky took to drinkin' harder an' harder, and was rabider an' rabider anti-coolie, but I don't think 'e was ever particularly glad that 'e *dispelled* Ah Wee. 'E didn't put on so much dog about it w'en we were alone as w'en 'e had the ear of a derned Spectacular *Extravaganza* like you. 'E put up that headstone and gouged the inscription accordin' to 'is varyin' moods. It took 'im three weeks, workin' between drinks. I gouged 'is in one day.

'When did Jo. die?' I asked rather absently. The answer took my breath:

'Pretty soon after I looked at 'im through that knot-hole, w'en you had put something in 'is w'isky, you derned Borgia!'

Recovering somewhat from my surprise at this *astounding* charge, I was half-minded to *throttl* the audacious accuser, but was restrained by a sudden *conviction* that came to me in the light of a revelation. I fixed a grave look upon him and asked, as calmly as I could: 'And when did you go loony?'

'Nine years ago!' he *shrieked,* throwing out his clenched hands -- 'nine years ago, w'en that big brute killed the woman who loved him better than she did me! -- me who had followed 'er from San Francisco, where 'e won 'er at draw poker! -- me who had watched over 'er for years w'en the scoundrel she belonged to was ashamed to acknowledge 'er and treat 'er white! -- me who for her sake kept 'is cussed secret till it ate 'im up! -- me who w'en you poisoned the beast fulfilled 'is last request to lay 'im *alongside* 'er and give 'im a stone to the head of 'im! And I've never since seen 'er grave till now, for I didn't want to meet 'im here.'

Grin - *A broad smile*
Dispelled - *Alleviate, vanish*
Extravaganza - *Lavish show*
Astounding - *Overwhelming*
Th ottle - *To choke suffocate*

'Meet him? Why, Gopher, my poor fellow, he is dead!'
'That's why I'm afraid of 'im.'

I followed the little wretch back to his wagon and *wrung* his hand at parting. It was now nightfall, and as I stood there at the roadside in the deepening *gloom*, watching the blank outlines of the *receding* wagon, a sound was borne to me on the evening wind -- a sound as of a series of *vigorous* thumps -- and a voice came out of the night:

'Gee-up, there, you derned old Geranium.'

Food For Thought

What had happened nine years ago? How did Jo. Dunfer kill the woman, whom Goher loved? Did Gopher kill Jo Dunfer? Why do you think that the author named the story as "The Haunted Valley"?

Wrung - *To twist forcibly*
Gloom - *Sadness, melancholy*
Receding - *Retreating*
Vigorous - *Energetic, forceful*

The Death of Halpin Frayser
— Ambrose Bierce

FOr by death is wrought greater change than hath been shown. Whereas in general the spirit that removed cometh back upon occasion, and is sometimes seen of those in flesh (appearing in the form of the body it bore) yet it hath happened that the *veritable* body without the spirit hath walked. And it is attested of those encountering who have lived to speak thereon that a lich so raised up hath no natural affection, nor remembrance thereof, but only hate. Also, it is known that some spirits which in life were benign become by death evil altogether. -- HALL.

One dark night in midsummer a man waking from a dreamless sleep in a forest lifted his head from the earth, and staring a few moments into the blackness, said: 'Catharine Larue.' He said nothing more; no reason was known to him why he should have said so much.

The man was Halpin Frayser. He lived in St. Helena, but where he lives now is uncertain, for he is dead. One who practises sleeping in the woods with nothing under him but the dry leaves and the damp earth, and nothing over him but the branches from which the leaves have fallen and the sky from which the earth has fallen, cannot hope for great longevity, and Frayser had already attained the age of thirty-two. There are persons in this world, millions of persons, and far and away the best persons, who regard that as a very advanced age. They are the children. To those who view the voyage of life from the port of departure the bark that has accomplished any considerable distance appears already in close approach to the farther shore. However, it is not certain that Halpin Frayser came to his death by *exposure*.

He had been all day in the hills west of the Napa Valley, looking for doves and such small game as was in season. Late in the afternoon it had come on to be cloudy, and he had lost his *bearings*; and although he had only to go always downhill -- everywhere the way to safety when one is lost -- the absence of trails had so *impeded* him that he was overtaken by night while still in the forest. Unable in the darkness to penetrate the *thickets* of manzanita and other undergrowth, **utterl**

Veritable - *Being truly*
Exposure - *Disclosure*
Bearings - *Th manner in which one conducts oneself*
Impeded - *Obstructed*
Thi kets - *Dense growth of shrubs, bushes*

bewildered and overcome with *fatigue*, he had lain down near the root of a large madrono and fallen into a dreamless sleep. It was hours later, in the very middle of the night, that one of God's *mysterious* messengers, gliding ahead of the incalculable host of his companions sweeping westward with the dawn line, pronounced the awakening word in the ear of the sleeper, who sat *upright* and spoke, he knew not why, a name, he knew not whose.

Halpin Frayser was not much of a philosopher, nor a scientist. The circumstance that, waking from a deep sleep at night in the midst of a forest, he had spoken aloud a name that he had not in memory and hardly had in mind did not arouse an enlightened curiosity to investigate the phenomenon. He thought it odd, and with a little *perfunctory* shiver, as if in deference to a seasonal presumption that the night was chill, he lay down again and went to sleep. But his sleep was no longer dreamless.

He thought he was walking along a dusty road that showed white in the gathering darkness of a summer night. *Whence* and whither it led, and why he travelled it, he did not know, though all seemed simple and natural, as is the way in dreams; for in the Land Beyond the Bed surprises cease from troubling and the judgment is at rest. Soon he came to a parting of the ways; leading from the highway was a road less travelled, having the appearance, indeed, of having been long abandoned, because, he thought, it led to something evil; yet he turned into it without hesitation, impelled by some imperious necessity.

As he pressed forward he became conscious that his way was haunted by invisible existences whom he could not definitely fiure to his mind. From among the trees on either side he caught broken and incoherent whispers in a strange tongue which yet he partly understood. They seemed to him fragmentary utteranc s of a monstrous *conspiracy* against his body and soul.

It was now long after nightfall, yet the interminable forest through which he journeyed was lit with a wan glimmer having no point of *diffusio* , for in its mysterious lumination nothing cast a shadow. A shallow pool in the guttered depression of an old wheel rut, as from a recent rain, met his eye with a crimson gleam. He *stooped* and *plunged* his hand into it. It stained his fingers; it was blood! Blood, he then observed, was about him everywhere. The weeds growing rankly by the roadside showed it in blots and

Fatigue - *Tiredness*
Upright - *Erect*
Perfunctory - *Superfic al*
Whence - *From what place, where*
Conspiracy - *Plotting*
Diffusion - *Verbosity*
Plunged - *To thrust forcible or suddenly*

splashes on their big, broad leaves. Patches of dry dust between the wheel-ways were pitted and spattered as with a red rain. *Defilin* the trunks of the trees were broad maculations of crimson, and blood dripped like dew from their foliage.

All this he observed with a terror which seemed not incompatible with the fulfilment of a natural expectation. It seemed to him that it was all in *expiation* of some crime which, though conscious of his guilt, he could not rightly remember. To the menaces and mysteries of his surroundings the consciousness was an added horror. Vainly he sought, by tracing life backward in memory, to reproduce the moment of his sin; scenes and incidents came crowding *tumultuously* into his mind, one picture effacing another, or *commingling* with it in confusion and obscurity, but nowhere could he catch a glimpse of what he sought. The failure *augmented* his terror; he felt as one who has murdered in the dark, not knowing whom nor why. So frightful was the situation -- the mysterious light burned with so silent and awful a *menace*; the noxious plants, the trees that by common consent are invested with a melancholy or baleful character, so openly in his sight conspired against his peace; from overhead and all about came so audible and startling whispers and the sighs of creatures so obviously not of earth -- that he could endure it no longer, and with a great effort to break some *malign* spell that bound his faculties to silence and inaction, he shouted with the full strength of his lungs! His voice, broken, it seemed, into an infinite multitude of unfamiliar sounds, went babbling and stammering away into the distant reaches of the forest, died into silence, and all was as before. But he had made a beginning at resistance and was encouraged. He said:

'I will not submit unheard. There may be powers that are not malignant travelling this accursed road. I shall leave them a record and an appeal. I shall relate my wrongs, the persecutions that I endure -- I, a helpless mortal, a penitent, an *unoffendin* poet!' Halpin Frayser was a poet only as he was a penitent: in his dream.

Taking from his clothing a small red-leather pocket-book one half of which was leaved for *memoranda*, he discovered that he was without a pencil. He broke a twig from a bush, dipped it into a pool of blood and wrote rapidly. He had hardly touched the paper with the point of his twig when a low, wild peal of

Defili g - *Making a narrow passage*
Expiation - *Atonement*
Tumultuously - *Highly agitated*
Commingling - *Combining, blending*
Augmented - *To make larger*
Memoranda - *A record, a written statement*

laughter broke out at a measureless distance away, and growing ever louder, seemed approaching ever nearer; a soulless, heartless, and unjoyous laugh, like that of the loon, solitary by the lakeside at midnight; a laugh which culminated in an unearthly shout close at hand, then died away by slow *gradations*, as if the *accursed* being that uttered it had withdrawn over the verge of the world whence it had come. But the man felt that this was not so -- that it was near by and had not moved.

A strange sensation began slowly to take possession of his body and his mind. He could not have said which, if any, of his senses was affected; he felt it rather as a consciousness -- a mysterious mental assurance of some overpowering presence -- some supernatural *malevolence* different in kind from the invisible existences that swarmed about him, and superior to them in power. He knew that it had uttered that hideous laugh. And now it seemed to be approaching him; from what direction he did not know -- dared not *conjecture*. All his former fears were forgotte or merged in the gigantic terror that now held him in thrall. Apart from that, he had but one thought: to complete his written appeal to the benign powers who, traversing the haunted wood, might sometime rescue him if he should be denied the blessing of *annihilation*. He wrote with terrible rapidity, the twig in his finger rilling blood without renewal; but in the middle of a sentence his hands denied their service to his will, his arms fell to his sides, the book to the earth; and powerless to move or cry out, he found himself staring into the sharply drawn face and blank, dead eyes of his own mother, standing white and silent in the garments of the grave!

II

In his youth Halpin Frayser had lived with his parents in Nashville, Tennessee. The Fraysers were well-to-do, having a good position in such society as had survived the wreck wrought by civil war. Their children had the social and educational opportunities of their time and place, and had responded to good associations and instruction with agreeable manners and cultivated minds. Halpin being the youngest and not over robust was perhaps a trifle 'spoiled.' He had the double disadvantage of a mother's *assiduity* and a father's neglect. Frayser pere was what no Southern man of means is not -- a politician. His coun-

Gradations - *Stages or degrees*
Accursed - *Ill-fated*
Annihilation - *Extinction, destruction*
Assiduity - *Devoled att ntion*

try, or rather his section and State, made demands upon his time and attention so *exacting* that to those of his family he was *compelled* to turn an ear partly *deafened* by the thunder of the political captains and the shouting, his own included.

Young Halpin was of a dreamy, indolent and rather romantic turn, somewhat more addicted to literature than law, the profession to which he was bred. Among those of his relations who professed the modern faith of heredity it was well understood that in him the character of the late Myron Bayne, a maternal great-grandfather, had revisited the glimpses of the moon -- by which orb Bayne had in his lifetime been sufficientl affected to be a poet of no small Colonial distinction. If not specially observed, it was observable that while a Frayser who was not the proud possessor of a *sumptuous* copy of the ancestral 'poetical works' (printed at the family expense, and long ago withdrawn from an inhospitable market) was a rare Frayser indeed, there was an illogical indisposition to honour the great deceased in the person of his spiritual successor. Halpin was pretty generally *deprecated* as an intellectual black sheep who was likely at any moment to disgrace the flock by bleating in metre. The Tennessee Fraysers were a practical folk -- not practical in the popular sense of devotion to *sordid pursuits*, but having a robust contempt for any qualities *unfitti* a man for the wholesome vocation of politics.

In justice to young Halpin it should be said that while in him were pretty faithfully reproduced most of the mental and moral characteristics ascribed by history and family tradition to the famous Colonial bard, his succession to the gift and faculty divine was purely *inferential*. Not only had he never been known to court the Muse, but in truth he could not have written correctly a line of verse to save himself from the Killer of the Wise. Still, there was no knowing when the dormant faculty might wake and *smite* the *lyre*.

In the meantime the young man was rather a loose fish anyhow. Between him and his mother was the most perfect sympathy, for secretly the lady was herself a *devout* disciple of the late and great Myron Bayne, though with the tact so generally and justly admired in her sex (despite the hardy *calumniators* who insist that it is essentially the same thing as cunning) she had always taken care to conceal her weakness from all eyes but those of him who shared

Sumptuous - *Luxurious*
Deprecated - *To express earnest disapproval*
Sordid - *Selfi h*
Inferential - *Pertaining to*
Smite - *To hit hard*
Lyre - *A musical instrument*
Calumniators - *People making false statements*

it. Their common guilt in respect of that was an added tie between them. If in Halpin's youth his mother had 'spoiled' him he had assuredly done his part toward being spoiled. As he grew to such manhood as is *attainabl* by a Southerner who does not care which way elections go, the attachmen between him and his beautiful mother -- whom from early childhood he had called Katy -- became yearly stronger and more tender. In these two romantic natures was manifest in a signal way that neglected phenomenon, the dominance of the sexual element in all the relations of life, strengthening, softening, and beautifying even those of consanguinity. The two were nearly inseparable, and by strangers observing their manners were not infrequently mistaken for lovers.

Entering his mother's boudoir one day Halpin Frayser kissed her upon the forehead, toyed for a moment with a lock of her dark hair which had escaped from its confining pins, and said, with an obvious effort at calmness:

'Would you greatly mind, Katy, if I were called away to California for a few weeks?'

It was hardly needful for Katy to answer with her lips a question to which her tell-tale cheeks had made instant reply. Evidently she would greatly mind; and the tears, too, sprang into her large brown eyes as *corroborative testimony.*

'Ah, my son,' she said, looking up into his face with infinit tenderness,' I should have known that this was coming. Did I not lie awake a half of the night weeping because, during the other half, Grandfather Bayne had come to me in a dream, and standing by his portrait -- young, too, and handsome as that -- pointed to yours on the same wall? And when I looked it seemed that I could not see the features; you had been painted with a face cloth, such as we put upon the dead. Your father has laughed at me, but you and I, dear, know that such things are not for nothing. And I saw below the edge of the cloth the marks of hands on your throat -- forgive me, but we have not been used to keep such things from each other. Perhaps you have another *interpretation*. Perhaps it does not mean that you will go to California. Or maybe you will take me with you?'

It must be confessed that this *ingenious* interpretation of the dream in the light of newly discovered evidence did not wholly *commend* itself to the son's more logical mind; he had, for the moment at least, a *conviction* that it foreshadowed a

---

Attainable - *Achievable*
Corroborative - *Confirmative*
Testimony - *A statement of declartion*
Interpretation - *Explanation*
Ingenious - *Bright, gift d*
Cmmend - *Praisen*

more simple and immediate, if less tragic, disaster than a visit to the Pacific Coast. It was Halpin Frayser's impression that he was to be *garroted* on his native heath.

'Are there not medicinal springs in California?' Mrs. Frayser resumed before he had time to give her the true reading of the dream -- 'places where one recovers from rheumatism and *neuralgia*? Look -- my fingers feel so stiff; and I am almost sure they have been giving me great pain while I slept.' She held out her hands for his inspection. What *diagnosis* of her case the young man may have thought it best to conceal with a smile the historian is unable to state, but for himself he feels bound to say that fingers looking less stiff, and showing fewer evidences of even insensible pain, have seldom been submitted for medical inspection by even the fairest patient desiring a prescription of unfamiliar scenes. The outcome of it was that of these two odd persons having equally odd notions of duty, the one went to California, as the interest of his client required, and the other remained at home in compliance with a wish that her husband was scarcely conscious of entertaining.

While in San Francisco Halpin Frayser was walking one dark night along the water-front of the city, when, with a suddenness that surprised and disconcerted him, he became a sailor. He was in fact '*shanghaied*' aboard a gallant, gallant ship, and sailed for a far countree. Nor did his misfortunes end with the voyage; for the ship was cast ashore on an island of the South Pacific, and it was six years afterward when the survivors were taken off by a venturesome trading schooner and brought back to San Francisco.

Though poor in purse, Frayser was no less proud in spirit than he had been in the years that seemed ages and ages ago. He would accept no assistance from strangers, and it was while living with a fellow survivor near the town of St. Helena, awaiting news and *remittance* from home, that he had gone gunning and dreaming.

III

The apparition *confronting* the dreamer in the haunted wood -- the thing so like, yet so unlike, his mother -- was horrible! It stirred no love nor *longings* insis heart; it came unattended with pleasant memories of a golden past --

Garroted - *To execute by the garrote, thrott e*
Neuralgia - *Sever pain due to nerve damage*
Diagnosis - *Determining*
Shanghaied - *To kidnap*
Remittances - *Sending of money*
Confronting - *Opposing*

Best Stories of Ambrose Bierce

inspired no sentiment of any kind; all the finer emotions were swallowed up in fear. He tried to turn and run from before it, but his legs were as lead; he was unable to lift his feet from the ground. His arms hung helpless at his sides; of his eyes only he retained control, and these he dared not remove from the *lustreless* orbs of the apparition, which he knew was not a soul without a body, but that most dreadful of all existences *infesting* that haunted wood -- a body without a soul! In its blank stare was neither love, nor pity, nor intelligence -- nothing to which to address an appeal for mercy. 'An appeal will not lie,' he thought, with an absurd reversion to professional slang, making the situation more horrible, as the fire of a cigar might light up a tomb

For a time, which seemed so long that the world grew grey with age and sin, and the haunted forest, having fulfille its purpose in this monstrous *culmination* of its terrors, vanished out of his consciousness with all its sights and sounds, the apparition stood within a pace, regarding him with the mindless *malevolence* of a wild brute; then thrust its hands forward and sprang upon him with *appalling ferocity*! The act released his physical energies without unfettering his will; his mind was still spellbound, but his powerful body and agile limbs, *endowed* with a blind, insensate life of their own, resisted *stoutly* and well. For an instant he seemed to see this unnatural contest between a dead intelligence and a breathing mechanism only as a spectator -- such fancies are in dreams; then he regained his identity almost as if by a leap forward into his body, and the straining automaton had a directing will as alert and fierce as that of its hideous antagonist.

But what mortal can cope with a creature of his dream? The imagination creating the enemy is already vanquished; the combat's result is the combat's cause. Despite his struggles -- despite his strength and activity, which seemed wasted in a void, he felt the cold fingers close upon his throat. Borne backward to the earth, he saw above him the dead and drawn face within a hand's-breadth of his own, and then all was black. A sound as of the beating of distant drums -- a murmur of *swarming* voices, a sharp, far cry signing all to silence, and Halpin Frayser dreamed that he was dead.

Lustreless - *Without sheen, dull*
Infesting - *Inhabit, overrun*
Culmination - *Result, ending*
Appalling - *Causing dismay or horror*
Stoutly - *Bravely*
Swarming - *To hover, congregate*

IV

A warm, clear night had been followed by a morning of *drenching* fog. At about the middle of the afternoon of the preceding day a little whiff of light vapour -- a mere thickening of the atmosphere, the ghost of a cloud -- had been observed *clinging* to the western side of Mount St. Helena, away up along the barren altitudes near the summit. It was so thin, so *diaphanous*, so like a fancy made visible, that one would have said: 'Look quickly! in a moment it will be gone.' In a moment it was visibly larger and denser. While with one edge it clung to the mountain, with the other it reached farther and farther out into the air above the lower slopes. At the same time it extended itself to north and south, joining small patches of mist that appeared to come out of the mountain-side on exactly the same level, with an intelligent design to be absorbed. And so it grew and grew until the summit was shut out of view from the valley, and over the valley itself was an ever-extending *canopy, opaque* and grey. At Calistoga, which lies near the head of the valley and the foot of the mountain, there were a starless night and a sunless morning. The fog, sinking into the valley, had reached southward, swallowing up ranch after ranch, until it had blotted out the town of St. Helena, nine miles away. The dust in the road was laid; trees were adrip with moisture; birds sat silent in their *coverts*; the morning light was wan and *ghastly*, with neither colour nor fire

Two men left the town of St. Helena at the first glimmer of dawn, and walked along the road north-ward up the valley toward Calistoga. They carried guns on their shoulders, yet no one having knowledge of such matters could have mistaken them for hunters of bird or beast. They were a deputy sheriff from Napa and a detective from San Francisco -- Holker and Jaralson, respectively. Their business was man-hunting.

'How far is it?' inquired Holker, as they strode along, their feet stirring white the dust beneath the damp surface of the road.

'The White Church? Only a half mile farther,' the other answered. 'By the way,' he added, 'it is neither white nor a church; it is an abandoned schoolhouse, grey with age and neglect. Religious services were once held in it -- when it was

Drenching - *To get wet thoroughly*
Diaphanous - *Completely transparently*
Canopy - *a covering*
Coverts - *Disguised*
Ghastly - *Terrible*

white, and there is a graveyard that would delight a poet. Can you guess why I sent for you, and told you to come armed?'

'Oh, I never have bothered you about things of that kind. I've always found you communicative when the time came. But if I may hazard a guess, you want me to help you arrest one of the corpses in the graveyard.'

'You remember Branscom?' said Jaralson, treating his companion's wit with the *inattentio* that it deserved.

'The chap who cut his wife's throat? I ought; I wasted a week's work on him and had my expenses for my trouble. There is a reward of fi e hundred dollars, but none of us ever got a sight of him. You don't mean to say -- '

'Yes, I do. He has been under the noses of you fellows all the time. He comes by night to the old graveyard at the White Church.'

'The devil! That's where they buried his wife.'

'Well, you fellows might have had sense enough to suspect that he would return to her grave some time!'

'The very last place that anyone would have expected him to return to.'

'But you had exhausted all the other places. Learning your failure at them, I "laid for him" there.'

'And you found him?'

'Damn it! he found me. The rascal got the drop on me -- regularly held me up and made me travel. It's God's mercy that he didn't go through me. Oh, he's a good one, and I fancy the half of that reward is enough for me if you're needy.'

Holker laughed good-humouredly, and explained that his *creditors* were never more *importunate*.

'I wanted merely to show you the ground, and arrange a plan with you,' the detective explained. 'I thought it as well for us to be armed, even in daylight.'

'The man must be *insane*,' said the deputy sheriff. 'The reward is for his capture and *conviction*. If he's mad he won't be convicted.'

Mr. Holker was so profoundly affected by that possible failure of justice that he involuntarily stopped in the middle of the road, then resumed his walk with *abated zeal.*

'Well, he looks it,' *assented* Jaralson. 'I'm bound to admit that a more *unshaven, unshorn, unkempt,* and uneverything

Creditors - *Persons or firms to whom money is due*
Importunate - *Urgent*
Insane - *Mad*
Abated - *To lesson*
Unshorn - *Unshaven*
Unkempt - *Uncared, neglected*

wretch I never saw outside the ancient and honourable order of tramps. But I've gone in for him, and can't make up my mind to let go. There's glory in it for us, anyhow. Not another soul knows that he is this side of the Mountains of the Moon.'

'All right,' Holker said; 'we will go and view the ground,' and he added, in the words of a once favourite inscription for tombstones: '"where you must shortly lie" -- I mean if old Branscom ever gets tired of you and your *impertinent intrusion*. By the way, I heard the other day that "Branscom" was not his real name.'

'What is?'

'I can't recall it. I had lost all interest in the wretch and it did not fix itself in my memory -- something like Pardee. The woman whose throat he had the bad taste to cut was a widow when he met her. She had come to California to look up some relatives -- there are persons who will do that sometimes. But you know all that.'

'Naturally.' 'But not knowing the right name, by what happy inspiration did you find the right grave? The man who told me what the name was said it had been cut on the headboard.'

'I don't know the right grave.' Jaralson was apparently a *trifle reluctant* to admit his ignorance of so important a point of his plan. 'I have been watching about the place generally. A part of our work this morning will be to identify that grave. Here is the White Church.'

For a long distance the road had been bordered by field on both sides, but now on the left there was a forest of oaks, madronos, and gigantic *spruces* whose lower parts only could be seen, dim and ghostly in the fog. The undergrowth was, in places, thick, but nowhere impenetrable. For some moments Holker saw nothing of the building, but as they turned into the woods it revealed itself in faint grey outline through the fog, looking huge and far away. A few steps more, and it was within an arm's length, distinct, dark with moisture, and insignificant in size. It had the usual country-schoolhouse form -- belonged to the packing-box order of architecture; had an *underpinning* of stones, a moss-grown roof, and blank window spaces, whence both glass and sash had long departed. It was ruined, but not a ruin -- a typical Californian substitute for what are known to guide-bookers

Impertinent - *Irrelevant entry*
Intrusion - *A forceful*
Trifle - *A thing*
Reluctant - *Unwilling*
Spruces - *Evergreen coniferous trees*
Underpinning - *Of little value*

abroad as 'monuments of the past.' With scarcely a glance at this uninteresting structure Jaralson moved on into the dripping undergrowth beyond.

'I will show you where he held me up,' he said. 'This is the graveyard.'

Here and there among the bushes were small *enclosures* containing graves, sometimes no more than one. They were recognised as graves by the discoloured stones or rotting boards at head and foot, *leaning* at all angles, some prostrate; by the ruined picket fences surrounding them; or, infrequently, by the mound itself showing its gravel through the fallen leaves. In many instances nothing marked the spot where lay the vestiges of some poor *mortal* -- who, leaving 'a large circle of sorrowing friends,' had been left by them in turn -- except a depression in the earth, more lasting than that in the spirits of the mourners. The paths, if any paths had been, were long obliterated; trees of a considerable size had been permitted to grow up from the graves and thrust aside with root or branch the *enclosing* fences. Over all was that air of abandonment and decay which seems nowhere so fit and significant as in a village of the forgotten dead.

As the two men, Jaralson leading, pushed their way through the growth of young trees, that *enterprising* man suddenly stopped and brought up his shotgun to the height of his breast, uttered a low note of warning, and stood motionless, his eyes fixed upon something ahead. As well as he could, *obstructed* by brush, his companion, though seeing nothing, imitated the posture and so stood, prepared for what might ensue. A moment later Jaralson moved *cautiously* forward, the other following.

Under the branches of an enormous spruce lay the dead body of a man. Standing silent above it they noted such particulars as first strike the attention -- the face, the attitude, the clothing; whatever most promptly and plainly answers the unspoken question of a sympathetic curiosity. The body lay upon its back, the legs wide apart. One arm was thrust upward, the other outward; but the latter was bent acutely, and the hand was near the throat. Both hands were tightly *clenched*. The whole attitude was that of desperate but *ineffectua resistance* to -- what?

Near by lay a shotgun and a game bag through the meshes of which was seen the *plumage* of shot birds. All about were

Enclosures - *Fencing*
Mortal - *Subject death*
Enterprising - *Resourceful, adventurous*
Clenched - *Grasped fi mly*
Plumage - *Feathers collectively*

evidences of a furious struggle; small sprouts of poison-oak were bent and *denuded* of leaf and bark; dead and rotting leaves had been pushed into heaps and ridges on both sides of the legs by the action of other feet than theirs; alongside the hips were unmistakable impressions of human knees.

The nature of the struggle was made clear by a glance at the dead man's throat and face. While breast and hands were white, those were purple -- almost black. The shoulders lay upon a low mound, and the head was turned back at an angle otherwise impossible, the expanded eyes staring blankly backward in a direction opposite to that of the feet. From the froth filling the open mouth the tongue *protruded*, black and swollen. The throat showed horrible *contusions*; not mere finger-marks, but *bruises* and *lacerations* wrought by two strong hands that must have buried themselves in the yielding flesh, maintaining their terrible grasp until long after death. Breast, throat, face, were wet; the clothing was saturated; drops of water, *condensed* from the fog, studded the hair and moustache.

All this the two men observed without speaking -- almost at a glance. Then Holker said:

'Poor devil! he had a rough deal.'

Jaralson was making a *vigilant circumspection* of the forest, his shotgun held in both hands and at full cock, his finger upon the trigger

'The work of a *maniac*,' he said, without withdrawing his eyes from the enclosing wood. 'It was done by Branscom -- Pardee.'

Something half hidden by the disturbed leaves on the earth caught Holker's attention. It was a redleather pocketbook. He picked it up and opened it. It contained leaves of white paper for *memoranda*, and upon the first leaf was the name 'Halpin Frayser.' Written in red on several succeeding leaves -- scrawled as if in haste and barely *legible* -- were the following lines, which Holker read aloud, while his companion continued *scanning* the dim grey confines of their narrow world and hearing matter of apprehension in the drip of water from every burdened branch:

> '*Enthralled* by some mysterious spell, I stood
> In the lit gloom of an enchanted wood.

Protruded - *Bulged, thrust forwards*
Bruises - *Slight injuries*
Lacerations - *Jagged wounds or outs*
Circumspection - *Cautious careful*
Maniac - *Crazy*
Scanning - *Examining*
Enthralled - *Captivated charmed*

The cypress there and myrtle twined their ***boughs***,
Significant, in ***baleful*** brotherhood.
'The brooding willow whispered to the yew;
Beneath, the deadly nightshade and the rue,
With ***immortelles*** self-woven into strange
Funereal shapes, and horrid nettles grew.
'No song of bird nor any drone of bees,
Nor light leaf lifted by the wholesome breeze:
The air was stagnant all, and Silence was
A living thing that breathed among the trees.
'***Conspiring*** spirits whispered in the gloom,
Half-heard, the stilly secrets of the tomb.
With blood the trees were all adrip; the leaves
Shone in the witch-light with a ***ruddy*** bloom.
'I cried aloud! -- the spell, unbroken still,
Rested upon my spirit and my will.
Unsouled, unhearted, hopeless and forlorn,
I strove with monstrous ***presages*** of ill!
'At last the viewless -- '

Holker ceased reading; there was no more to read. The manuscript broke off in the middle of a line.

'That sounds like Bayne,' said Jaralson, who was something of a scholar in his way. He had ***abated*** his vigilance and stood looking down at the body.

'Who's Bayne?' Holker asked rather incuriously.

'Myron Bayne, a chap who flourished in the early years of the nation -- more than a century ago. Wrote mighty dismal stuff; I have his collected works. That poem is not among them, but it must have been omitted by mistake.'

'It is cold,' said Holker; 'let us leave here; we must have up the coroner from Napa.'

Jaralson said nothing, but made a movement in compliance. Passing the end of the slight elevation of earth upon which the dead man's head and shoulders lay, his foot struck some hard substance under the rotting forest leaves, and he took the trouble to kick it into view. It was a fallen headboard, and painted on it were the hardly ***decipherable*** words, 'Catharine Larue.'

Funereal - *Mournful, gloomy*
Conspiring - *Plott ng against*
Presages - *Prophetic*
Ruddy - *Damned*
Decipherable - *To interpret, depictable, portrayable*

'Larue, Larue!' exclaimed Holker, with sudden animation. 'Why, that is the real name of Branscom -- not Pardee. And -- bless my soul! how it all comes to me -- the murdered woman's name had been Frayser!'

'There is some rascally mystery here,' said Detective Jaralson. 'I hate anything of that kind.' There came to them out of the fog -- seemingly from a great distance -- the sound of a laugh, a low, *deliberate*, soulless laugh which had no more of joy than that of a hyena *night-prowling* in the desert; a laugh that rose by slow gradation, louder and louder, clearer, more distinct and terrible, until it seemed barely outside the narrow circle of their vision; a laugh so unnatural, so unhuman, so *devilish*, that it filled those hardy man-hunters with a sense of dread *unspeakable*! They did not move their weapons nor think of them; the menace of that horrible sound was not of the kind to be met with arms. As it had grown out of silence, so now it died away; from a *culminating* shout which had seemed almost in their ears, it drew itself away into the distance until its failing notes, joyous and *mechanical* to the last, sank to silence at a measureless remove.

Food For Thought

Some literary critics feel that the ending of this story is very sporadic and confusing. How do you feel about it? Do you think that the story could have a better ending? Suggest one suitable ending of this story, using your own imaginative skills.

Deliberate -
Night - Prowling -
Devilish -
Unspeakable -
Mechanical -

SELF-IMPROVEMENT/PERSONALITY DEVELOPMENT

   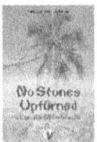    

Also Available in Hindi   Also Available in Hindi   Also Available in Kannada, Tamil

Also Available in Kannada

Also Available in Kannada

STRESS MANAGEMENT

All books available at www.vspublishers.com

RELIGION/SPIRITUALITY/ASTROLOGY/PALMISTRY/PALMISTRY/VASTU/HYPNOTISM

CAREER & BUSINESS MANAGEMENT

Also Available in Hindi, Kannada

     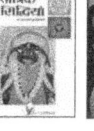

Also Available in Hindi, Kannada

Also Available in Kannada

Contact us at sales@vspublishers.com

QUIZ BOOKS

ENGLISH IMPROVEMENT

ACTIVITIES BOOK

QUOTES/SAYINGS

BIOGRAPHIES

     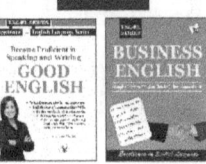

IELTS TECH

CHILDREN SCIENCE LIBRARY

COMPUTER BOOKS

All books available at www.vspublishers.com

www.ingramcontent.com/pod-product-compliance
Lightning Source LLC
Chambersburg PA
CBHW070500100426
42743CB00010B/1705